LEARN AIRFLOW

Master Data Orchestration with Technical Precision

Diego Rodrigues

LEARN AIRFLOW
Master Data Orchestration with Technical Precision

2025 Edition

Author: Diego Rodrigues

studiod21portoalegre@gmail.com

Published by StudioD21.

Important Note

The code and scripts presented in this book are primarily intended to practically illustrate the concepts discussed throughout the chapters. They were developed to demonstrate didactic applications in controlled environments and may therefore require adaptations to work correctly in different contexts. It is the reader's responsibility to validate the specific configurations of their development environment before practical implementation.

More than providing ready-made solutions, this book seeks to encourage a solid understanding of the fundamentals covered, promoting critical thinking and technical autonomy. The examples presented should be seen as starting points for the reader to develop their own original solutions adapted to the real demands of their career or projects. True technical competence arises from the ability to internalize essential principles and apply them creatively, strategically, and transformatively.

We therefore encourage each reader to go beyond simply reproducing the examples, using this content as a foundation to build their own scripts and codes, capable of generating significant impact in their professional trajectory. This is the spirit of applied knowledge: learning deeply to innovate with purpose.

Thank you for your trust, and we wish you a productive and inspiring learning journey.

CONTENTS

GREETINGS

It is with great objectivity and clarity that I welcome you as you embark on this journey through the world of data orchestration with Apache Airflow. Your decision to understand and apply this tool represents a conscious step toward more organized, auditable, and scalable data environments — a practical choice in response to the real operational needs of those working with automation, data engineering, or critical pipelines.

In this book, LEARN AIRFLOW – Master Data Orchestration with Technical Precision, you will find direct, functional content built with total focus on applicability. Airflow has ceased to be an alternative solution and has become an integral part of modern data architectures. By understanding how it works, you not only control technical executions but also the reliability of entire processes that drive products, reports, decisions, and business flows.

Here, you will be guided by a solid structure, where each chapter has been planned to connect applied theory with validated practice. The goal is not to present the tool superficially, but to guide its professional use in real contexts — from creating basic DAGs to scalable deployment with Kubernetes, integration with external APIs, management of sensitive variables, auditing, versioning, and continuous observability.

This work does not require you to be an expert to start, but it does require — and delivers — technical rigor. If you work with data and need predictability, automation, and governance over recurring processes, mastering Airflow becomes an immediate differentiator.

Whether you are an engineer, analyst, data scientist, DevOps professional, or solutions architect, this content was designed to assist you with precision and focus. The 25 chapters that make up this book directly address everything necessary to operate Airflow in production environments, across multiple settings, with security and traceability.

Practical knowledge begins with clear structure — and this reading was crafted exactly for that.

Welcome to Learn Airflow. Enjoy your reading and application.

ABOUT THE AUTHOR

Diego Rodrigues
Technical Author and Independent Researcher
ORCID: https://orcid.org/0009-0006-2178-634X
StudioD21 Smart Tech Content & Intell Systems
E-mail: studiod21portoalegre@gmail.com
LinkedIn: www.linkedin.com/in/diegoxpertai

An international technical author (tech writer) focused on structured production of applied knowledge. He is the founder of StudioD21 Smart Tech Content & Intell Systems, where he leads the creation of intelligent frameworks and the publication of didactic technical books supported by artificial intelligence, such as the Kali Linux Extreme series, SMARTBOOKS D21, among others.

Holder of 42 international certifications issued by institutions such as IBM, Google, Microsoft, AWS, Cisco, META, Ec-Council, Palo Alto, and Boston University, he operates in the fields of Artificial Intelligence, Machine Learning, Data Science, Big Data, Blockchain, Connectivity Technologies, Ethical Hacking, and Threat Intelligence.

Since 2003, he has developed more than 200 technical projects for brands in Brazil, the USA, and Mexico. In 2024, he established himself as one of the leading technical authors of the new generation, with more than 180 titles published in six languages. His work is based on his proprietary TECHWRITE 2.2 applied technical writing protocol, focused on scalability, conceptual precision, and practical applicability in professional

DIEGO RODRIGUES

environments.

BOOK PRESENTATION

This book has been organized to offer clear and direct technical guidance on using Apache Airflow, from introducing its core concepts to applications in complex and scalable environments. Across 25 chapters, the reader will be guided through a didactic sequence that balances applied theory, recommended practices, and realistic examples.

We start with the fundamentals, covering the first steps in installing Airflow, creating users, directory structure, and initializing essential components such as the scheduler and the webserver. Next, we show how to create your first DAG, explaining the function of each parameter, the initial scheduling, the use of basic operators, and the importance of task chaining.

We then move on to the use of the most common operators — such as BashOperator, PythonOperator, and EmailOperator — and demonstrate how to configure them correctly for everyday tasks. Shortly after, we address the use of variables and connections, teaching how to parameterize DAGs securely and reuse configurations across tasks and environments.

We continue into conditional execution logic through trigger rules, presenting different dependency rules between tasks, and follow with an explanation of scheduling in Airflow, detailing start_date, schedule_interval, catchup, and the behavior of execution_date. With this, the reader gains a clear view of how to control execution timing.

In the following chapters, we dive into communication between tasks using XComs, then into building conditional flows using BranchPythonOperator. We introduce sensors such as FileSensor, HttpSensor, and ExternalTaskSensor, showing how to wait for external events before proceeding in the pipeline. We also explain how to monitor DAGs and tasks through the web interface, interpret logs, and use the available graphical visualizations.

The content then moves into customizations with the creation of custom operators and hooks, allowing encapsulation of business logic and structured connection of Airflow to internal systems. With this, we lay the groundwork for scalability topics: we show how to configure the tool's parallelism, control execution concurrency, and distribute the load using pools.

We dedicate a full chapter to deploying Airflow with Docker, including volume configuration, environment variables, and the use of Docker Compose to replicate local environments. Next, we detail the use of the Kubernetes Executor, with pod templates and automatic task-level scalability. We complement this technical section with integration with Spark and Hadoop, exploring the SparkSubmitOperator and connecting to HDFS for large data volumes.

From there, we present ways to integrate Airflow with external APIs through the SimpleHttpOperator, illustrating both sending and consuming data via REST. In the chapter on testing and debugging, we guide the use of airflow tasks test, log analysis, and debugging with breakpoints in IDEs like VS Code.

We continue with the use of Jinja templates and macros, fundamental for making tasks dynamic and adaptable to runtime. Next, we address the tool's security mechanisms: authentication, access control with RBAC, variable protection, and secure configuration best practices.

In the external automation section, we show how to use Airflow's REST API to trigger DAGs, query executions, create variables, and manage connections via HTTP. This flow connects directly to the chapter on versioning, where we explain how to control DAGs with Git, structure branches by environment, and configure CI/CD pipelines for automated deployment.

With the reader already prepared for distributed environments, we introduce the Celery Executor, explaining its architecture with Redis or RabbitMQ as brokers, load balancing among workers, and performance tuning. We then detail the use of remote logging with S3, GCS, and ELK, as well as strategies for auditing and log retention.

In the final chapters, we address real-world orchestration cases with multiple environments, team integration, and standardization of critical flows. Finally, we close with continuous monitoring practices, the creation of healthchecks, alerts with Slack and PagerDuty, exposure of metrics via Prometheus, and the construction of technical dashboards with Grafana.

This book not only teaches how Airflow works. It guides, chapter by chapter, how to use the tool consciously, predictably, and in alignment with the demands of real operations. The structure is designed to offer the reader clarity, context, and direct application — with precise, modular, and rigorously practical language.

CHAPTER 1. GETTING STARTED WITH APACHE AIRFLOW

Apache Airflow is a workflow orchestration tool that allows you to automate data pipelines, modeling each stage of the flow as code. This chapter aims to set up the local Airflow execution environment, configure the platform's initial elements, and present its essential structural concepts. The approach will be straightforward, with functional commands and a focus on the real use of the tool.

Basic Execution with Code

Airflow should be installed inside a Python virtual environment to ensure dependency isolation. The first step is to create this environment with venv:

bash

```
python -m venv airflow_venv
```

Activate the environment:

bash

```
source airflow_venv/bin/activate # Linux/macOS
airflow_venv\Scripts\activate    # Windows
```

With the environment activated, install Apache Airflow with the specific constraints:

bash

```
pip install apache-airflow==2.7.2 --constraint "https://
raw.githubusercontent.com/apache/airflow/constraints-2.7.2/
constraints-3.8.txt"
```

Initialize Airflow's internal database:

bash

```
airflow db init
```

Create the first administrative user for authentication in the Web interface:

bash

```
airflow users create \
    --username admin \
    --firstname Admin \
    --lastname User \
    --role Admin \
    --email admin@example.com
```

Start Airflow's essential services:

bash

```
airflow webserver --port 8080
```

Then, in a new terminal window:

bash

```
airflow scheduler
```

With this, the environment will be accessible at http://localhost:8080 with the defined credentials.

Functional Variations

Airflow can be installed with specific extras for certain connectors and operators. For example, for PostgreSQL and Google Cloud support:

bash

```
pip install "apache-airflow[postgres,google]"
```

In addition to local installation, Airflow can be configured with Docker using docker-compose, which allows replicating environments and simplifying deployment. This approach is recommended for team testing or staging environments.

The default backend in local environments is SQLite, which does not support concurrent execution. In production, PostgreSQL or MySQL should be used as the backend, and Redis or RabbitMQ as the broker.

System Behavior

Airflow stores its metadata in a relational database. Running the command below creates tables that store DAGs, tasks, logs, variables, and connections:

bash

```
airflow db init
```

The scheduler periodically checks the DAG files, interprets the execution definitions, and schedules tasks according to the defined criteria. Each task has its status recorded and continuously updated. The webserver displays all this information in the graphical interface, allowing detailed monitoring.

By default, DAGs should be located in the directory:

bash

~/airflow/dags/

When a DAG is saved in this directory, the scheduler detects, interprets, and automatically registers its existence, provided there is no syntax or import error.

Control and Monitoring

After installation and initial configuration, it is possible to check the installation status with:

bash

airflow info

This command returns details such as version, installation path, environment settings, and component status.

To check if the DAGs are being correctly recognized:

bash

airflow dags list

To list the tasks of a specific DAG:

bash

airflow tasks list dag_name

The Web interface also allows viewing the status of each DAG, execution time, task statuses, and detailed logs.

Logs can be accessed directly through the interface or the file system in the default directory:

bash

```
~/airflow/logs/
```

Common Error Resolution

DAG does not appear in the Web interface
Check if the file is in the correct directory (`~/airflow/dags/`) and if there is no import or syntax error in the DAG code.

Scheduler does not execute tasks
Ensure that the scheduler is running and that the DAG's schedule time is compatible with the start_date configuration.

Webserver does not start
It may be necessary to run airflow db init again or review the permissions of the configuration files.

Authentication error in the interface
Recreate the user with the command airflow users create, ensuring the correct definition of password and email.

Error using SQLite with multiple instances
SQLite does not support concurrent read/write. Use PostgreSQL in environments with multiple workers.

Best Practices

- Install Airflow in an isolated virtual environment

- Use official constraints during installation

- Check logs after any DAG loading failure

- Replace SQLite with PostgreSQL in shared environments

- Create users with well-defined roles for access control

Strategic Summary

This first chapter presented the complete process for local installation of Apache Airflow with Python, initial environment setup, user creation, and activation of the main services: webserver and scheduler. The fundamental concepts of the tool were also introduced, such as DAGs, tasks, directory structure, and Web interface access. With this knowledge established, the reader is ready to define their first DAGs in the next chapter, beginning the automation of real pipelines with Airflow.

CHAPTER 2. CREATING YOUR FIRST DAG

This chapter introduces the creation of the first DAG (Directed Acyclic Graph) in Apache Airflow, demonstrating how to define the task flow in Python, the essential configuration parameters, and the inclusion of multiple sequential tasks. By the end, the reader will be able to manually execute the pipeline, visualize it in the graphical interface, and understand the interaction between the scheduler, DAG, and task execution.

Basic Execution with Code

Every DAG is a Python file saved in the dags/ directory. The minimum structure requires importing the main modules and defining a DAG object with its tasks.
Create a file named primeira_dag.py in the ~/airflow/dags/ directory with the following content:

python

```
from airflow import DAG

from airflow.operators.python import PythonOperator

from datetime import datetime


def tarefa_exemplo():
    print("Executing example task")


with DAG(
```

```python
    dag_id='minha_primeira_dag',
    start_date=datetime(2024, 1, 1),
    schedule_interval=None,
    catchup=False,
    tags=['example']
) as dag:

    tarefa1 = PythonOperator(
        task_id='execute_task',
        python_callable=tarefa_exemplo
    )
```

This code defines a DAG without a schedule (schedule_interval=None), with only one task executing a Python function.

To manually execute the DAG via terminal:

bash

```bash
airflow dags trigger minha_primeira_dag
```

To visualize the execution:

bash

```bash
airflow tasks list minha_primeira_dag
```

Follow the status on the Web interface: http://localhost:8080

Functional Variations

It is possible to include multiple chained tasks to simulate a simple pipeline. Below is an example with three sequential tasks:

python

```python
def task_1():
    print("Start of the pipeline")


def task_2():
    print("Intermediate processing")


def task_3():
    print("Pipeline completion")


with DAG(
    dag_id='simple_pipeline',
    start_date=datetime(2024, 1, 1),
    schedule_interval=None,
    catchup=False
) as dag:

    t1 = PythonOperator(
        task_id='start',
        python_callable=task_1
    )
```

```
t2 = PythonOperator(
    task_id='processing',
    python_callable=task_2
)


t3 = PythonOperator(
    task_id='end',
    python_callable=task_3
)


t1 >> t2 >> t3
```

The >> operator defines the execution order between tasks. This DAG can be manually triggered, and all steps will execute in the defined sequence.

System Behavior

When the DAG file is saved, the scheduler automatically detects its presence. The system checks if the DAG has a unique dag_id, a valid start_date, and correctly defined tasks. Airflow validates the file's syntax, registers it in the metadata database, and displays it in the graphical interface.

Tasks executed manually are registered as "triggered runs" and displayed with execution date and status. Each task generates logs stored in:

bash

```
~/airflow/logs/<dag_id>/<task_id>/<execution_date>/
```

The transition between tasks follows the defined acyclic graph, and each step only runs after the previous one has successfully completed.

Control and Monitoring

After triggering the DAG, you can monitor the execution directly through the Web interface. In the side menu, click on DAGs, then select simple_pipeline and click on "Graph View" to see the task order.

The "Trigger DAG" button allows you to manually start the execution. The "Refresh" button forces reading of the DAG files, useful after making changes.

Each task has a "Log" button, which displays the Python function's output, including prints and error messages.

To monitor via terminal:

bash

```
airflow tasks list simple_pipeline
airflow tasks test simple_pipeline start 2024-01-01
```

This second command allows testing an isolated task in a simulated context.

Common Error Resolution

DAG does not appear in the interface
Check if the file name ends with .py and is saved in the correct directory (~/airflow/dags/).

Import error in the Python file
Ensure all imports are correct, especially DAG and PythonOperator.

Task does not execute after manual trigger
Review the DAG's start_date and ensure catchup is set to False.

Error message "Task is not mapped"
Check if the task was correctly added to the with DAG(...) as dag block.

Execution stuck at "queued"
Ensure the scheduler is running and there are no conflicts with other running DAGs.

Best Practices

- Name DAGs and tasks descriptively and consistently

- Avoid future start_date values to simplify local testing

- Use catchup=False to avoid unwanted retroactive executions

- Include tags in DAGs for organization in the interface

- Isolate each DAG in a single Python file in the dags/ directory

Strategic Summary

In this chapter, the first functional DAG was created in Apache Airflow. The reader learned how to structure sequential tasks, define essential DAG parameters, manually execute the pipeline, and monitor its execution via the Web interface. This foundation will enable, in the following chapters, deeper use of native operators, dependency rules, advanced parameters, and integrations with external environments. Mastering DAG creation is the first step to orchestrating data pipelines with full control over each stage.

CHAPTER 3. ESSENTIAL OPERATORS IN AIRFLOW

Airflow organizes task execution through operators. Each operator represents a specific action that will be performed within a DAG. The most used operators are BashOperator, PythonOperator, and EmailOperator, each with different behaviors, requirements, and applications, but all follow the same principle: encapsulating the execution logic of a pipeline stage.

Correct construction of operators and effective chaining between them is the core of a functional DAG. Understanding the particularities of each type is essential to ensure that the flow behaves as expected, without failures, rework, or system overload.

BashOperator, PythonOperator, EmailOperator

The BashOperator runs commands directly in the system shell. It is ideal for simple tasks such as file copies, shell script calls, running local tools, or external commands that do not require conditional logic in Python.
Basic example with BashOperator:

python

```
from airflow.operators.bash import BashOperator


command = BashOperator(
    task_id='shell_command',
```

```
    bash_command='echo "Running via BashOperator"',
    dag=dag
)
```

The `bash_command` parameter defines the instruction to be executed in the shell. This command will be triggered when the operator is called in the DAG.

The PythonOperator is used to execute Python functions directly. It is the most flexible operator and frequently used in pipelines with business logic, transformations, validations, and interactions with custom libraries.

python

```
from airflow.operators.python import PythonOperator


def process_data():
    print("Processing with Python")


python_task = PythonOperator(
    task_id='python_task',
    python_callable=process_data,
    dag=dag
)
```

The `python_callable` must always be a function, not the result of calling the function. It will run internally in the DAG context with arguments like **kwargs, if desired.

The EmailOperator is used to send emails directly from a task. It can be used for alerts, reports, and execution confirmations.

python

```
from airflow.operators.email import EmailOperator

email = EmailOperator(
    task_id='send_email',
    to='user@example.com',
    subject='Execution Completed',
    html_content='<p>The DAG was successfully completed.</p>',
    dag=dag
)
```

This operator requires that the email backend is correctly configured in airflow.cfg, including SMTP server, port, user, and password, or the equivalent setup in airflow.yaml.

Required Parameters and Typical Usage

All operators inherit from the BaseOperator class and share certain essential parameters:

- task_id: Unique task identifier within the DAG

- dag: Reference to the DAG object it belongs to (can be omitted if inside the with block)

- depends_on_past: Defines whether the task depends on the success of the previous execution

- retries: Number of retry attempts in case of failure

- retry_delay: Interval between retry attempts

Additionally, each operator has specific parameters. The BashOperator requires bash_command, the PythonOperator requires python_callable, and the EmailOperator requires to, subject, and html_content.

Typical use involves defining multiple operators with distinct functions and chaining them to compose the pipeline.

Chaining Tasks with Different Operators

The most common way to chain tasks in Airflow is using the flow operators >> and <<. They indicate the execution order between tasks:

python

```
task1 >> task2 >> task3
```

Or using the methods set_downstream and set_upstream:

python

```
task1.set_downstream(task2)
```

Mixing different operators in a DAG is common and recommended. For example, you can use a BashOperator to extract data, a PythonOperator to process it, and an EmailOperator to notify the team.

python

```
extract = BashOperator(...)

transform = PythonOperator(...)

notify = EmailOperator(...)
```

extract >> transform >> notify

Execution Behavior

During execution, each operator is interpreted by the scheduler, which places the task in the execution queue according to the defined schedule and DAG logic. The executor (for example, SequentialExecutor, LocalExecutor, CeleryExecutor) treats each operator as an autonomous unit.

The BashOperator opens a shell subprocess on the worker and executes the command. The standard output is captured in the logs. The PythonOperator executes the function directly in the worker process. The EmailOperator triggers a connection to the SMTP server and sends the email.

In case of failure, the operators follow the defined retry policy, store error logs, and change the task status to failed, up_for_retry, or skipped, depending on the configuration.

The correct combination between operators should consider:

- Expected execution time

- Impact on worker resources

- External network dependency (such as SMTP in EmailOperator)

- Log size and sensitivity of transmitted information

Common Error Resolution

Import error for operator

Check if you are using the correct import path, such as from airflow.operators.bash import BashOperator or from airflow.operators.python import PythonOperator.

Task does not execute correctly
Ensure all required parameters are defined and that the operator is associated with a valid DAG.

Encoding problem in shell commands
Include explicit encodings in BashOperator when using accents or special characters.

Failure to send email
Review the SMTP settings in the airflow.cfg file or set appropriate environment variables.

Task silently fails without useful log
Ensure the PythonOperator function does not contain silent errors such as empty returns or unhandled exceptions.

Best Practices

- Use Airflow's native operators whenever possible, avoiding unnecessary external scripts

- Name operators with descriptive and consistent task_id

- Separate complex Python logic outside the DAG file

- Manually test BashOperator commands before including them in the DAG

- Validate email configuration with tests outside Airflow before using EmailOperator

Strategic Summary

Operators are the execution foundation of DAGs in Airflow. Correct use of BashOperator, PythonOperator, and EmailOperator allows creating robust, flexible, and monitorable flows. Understanding the parameters, chaining methods, and execution behavior gives full control over each pipeline stage. The proper choice of operator for each task directly impacts the reliability and efficiency of orchestration. The foundation is now set to move forward into variables and connections in the next stage of building smart pipelines.

CHAPTER 4. WORKING WITH VARIABLES AND CONNECTIONS

Managing variables and connections in Apache Airflow is fundamental to creating reusable, secure, and scalable DAGs. These two features allow configuration to be decoupled from code, simplify maintenance, and promote pipeline portability across different environments. Variables store dynamic values accessible within tasks, while connections centralize credentials and access data for external systems such as databases, APIs, storage buckets, and cloud services.

Creating Variables in the Airflow UI

Airflow has an intuitive graphical interface for creating and managing variables. To access this functionality, click on "Admin" in the top menu and then on "Variables." You can create a new variable by clicking "+" in the top-right corner.

Each variable consists of a Key and a Value. This structure allows you to centralize configurations that can be read within DAG code using the Variable module. You can

store simple text, directory paths, connection strings, API tokens, or even JSON objects, as long as they are properly formatted.

The interface also allows importing and exporting variables in JSON format. This simplifies replication between development, staging, and production environments.

Secure Storage of Credentials

Variables should not be used to store passwords or sensitive tokens directly, even though this is technically possible. Airflow provides more appropriate mechanisms for that: connections, which support "hidden" fields and store data encrypted in the metadata database.

When using variables with sensitive information, it is necessary to configure encryption in airflow.cfg with a valid fernet_key. This key allows Airflow to automatically encrypt values before storage and decrypt only at the time of DAG reading. Even so, best practice is to delegate this type of data to connections, which are natively designed for this purpose.

It is recommended to enable the setting hide_sensitive_var_conn_fields = True in airflow.cfg to avoid accidental exposure of credentials in the Web interface or logs.

Using the Variable Module

The airflow.models.Variable module allows accessing variables directly in the DAG's Python code. To do this, you must import the module and use the get method.

Example usage:

python

```
from airflow.models import Variable


data_path = Variable.get("base_data_path")
```

This command retrieves the value associated with the base_data_path key and stores it in the Python variable data_path.

It is also possible to define a default value, which is returned if the variable does not exist:

python

```
endpoint = Variable.get("api_endpoint", default_var="https://
```

api.default.com")

For variables in JSON format:

python

```
parameters = Variable.get("batch_parameters",
deserialize_json=True)
```

This approach is useful for storing multiple parameters in a single record, optimizing management and versioning.

Configuring Connections (Connection IDs)

Connections in Airflow represent integrations with external sources. Each connection has a unique ID (conn_id) that will be referenced in the DAG. Connections are accessed via the "Admin" > "Connections" menu.

When creating a new connection, fill in the fields:

- **Conn Id**: identifier used in DAGs

- **Conn Type**: type of connection (Postgres, MySQL, HTTP, Amazon S3, etc.)

- **Host, Schema, Login, Password, Port**: specific connection data

- **Extra**: optional JSON field with additional parameters

Model PostgreSQL connection:

- Conn Id: postgres_analytics

- Conn Type: Postgres

- **Host:** 10.0.1.55

- **Schema:** public_data

- **Login:** admin

- **Password:** SecurePassword123

- **Port:** 5432

In the DAG code, the connection is referenced through operators that support this type of integration. Example with the PostgresOperator:

python

```
from airflow.providers.postgres.operators.postgres import PostgresOperator


run_sql = PostgresOperator(
    task_id='query_database',
    postgres_conn_id='postgres_analytics',
    sql='SELECT * FROM sales',
    dag=dag
)
```

Airflow handles the credentials correctly, avoiding the exposure of sensitive information in the code.

Connections can also be created via command line:

bash

```
airflow connections add 'my_database' \
```

```
--conn-uri 'postgresql://user:password@host:5432/schema'
```

This practice allows configuration automation in continuous deployment environments.

Common Error Resolution

Variable not found in code
Ensure that the key typed in Variable.get() exactly matches the one registered in the interface. Airflow is case-sensitive.

JSON decoding error using deserialize_json=True
Make sure the variable's value is valid JSON. Avoid extra commas and incorrect quotation marks.

Password visible in interface or logs
Avoid storing credentials in variables. Prefer connections with hidden fields and encryption enabled.

Connection fails when executing operator
Check the filled fields in the connection configuration. Ensure that the Conn Id exactly matches the value used in the operator.

Malformed extra field
The extra field must contain valid JSON. Use validation tools before saving the configuration.

Best Practices

- Use variables only for configuration data, not for secrets

- Centralize all file paths and endpoints in variables with standardized names

- Create clearly named connections, separated by environment and purpose

- Enable encryption with fernet_key to protect sensitive data

- Avoid hardcoding parameters in the DAG code; use Variable or Connection whenever possible

Strategic Summary

The use of variables and connections in Apache Airflow promotes organization, reusability, and security in data pipelines. Variables allow parameterizing tasks without changing the code, while connections centralize credentials and reduce the risk of exposing sensitive data. Mastery of these tools ensures portability across environments and simplifies the maintenance of complex DAGs. The combination of both resources results in cleaner, more professional workflows prepared for continuous operation in production environments.

CHAPTER 5. TRIGGER RULES AND DEPENDENCIES

The execution of tasks in an Airflow DAG does not depend only on the sequence in which they were declared, but also on trigger rules. These criteria control when a task can be executed based on the status of previous tasks. Understanding and correctly configuring dependencies and execution rules is essential for building robust, fault-tolerant, and adaptable data flows for complex scenarios.

Definition of Execution Rules

By default, a task in Airflow will only run if all its upstream tasks succeed. This behavior is defined by the all_success rule, which is the system's default trigger rule. However, there are many other control modes that allow tasks to run even when there are upstream failures, as long as certain conditions are met.

The main available trigger rules are:

- all_success: runs the task only if all upstream tasks succeed

- all_failed: runs only if all upstream tasks fail

- all_done: runs regardless of upstream task outcomes

- one_success: runs if at least one upstream task succeeds

- one_failed: runs if at least one upstream task fails

- none_failed: runs if no upstream task fails (even if some were skipped)

- none_failed_or_skipped: runs if no upstream task fails or is skipped

- none_skipped: runs if no upstream task was skipped

- dummy: used for tasks that should not execute, only for logical chaining

These rules can be assigned directly in the task definition using the trigger_rule argument.

Using trigger_rule in Real Context

In pipelines involving optional steps or conditional logic, execution rules are fundamental. A common case is sending alerts only if there are prior failures.

python

```
from airflow.operators.email import EmailOperator
from airflow.utils.trigger_rule import TriggerRule


failure_alert = EmailOperator(
    task_id='send_alert',
    to='devops@company.com',
    subject='Pipeline Error',
    html_content='One of the tasks has failed.',
    trigger_rule=TriggerRule.ONE_FAILED,
    dag=dag
)
```

In this example, the email operator will run if at least one previous task fails. This avoids unnecessary alerts and keeps focus on problematic runs.

Another common scenario is the use of cleanup tasks, which should always run regardless of the success or failure of prior steps. For this, use all_done.

python

```python
cleanup = PythonOperator(
    task_id='clean_temp_files',
    python_callable=clean_temp,
    trigger_rule='all_done',
    dag=dag
)
```

Configuring Conditional Dependencies

Beyond setting execution rules, it is possible to chain tasks conditionally, controlling the flow based on the outcome of prior tasks. A common feature is the use of BranchPythonOperator, which allows choosing the DAG's path based on a logical decision.

python

```python
from airflow.operators.python import BranchPythonOperator


def choose_path():
    if check_condition():
        return 'task_path_a'
```

```
    else:
        return 'task_path_b'

branch = BranchPythonOperator(
    task_id='decide_flow',
    python_callable=choose_path,
    dag=dag
)
```

The function's return must be the task_id of the next task to be executed. Other tasks will automatically be skipped, and trigger rules become crucial for downstream tasks to know when they should run, even with skipped paths.

You can also combine multiple paths using dummy or empty operators to consolidate the flow into a final task.

Failure Interpretation in Chaining

Failures in intermediate tasks directly affect the execution of subsequent steps. When a task fails, its status is recorded as failed. If a downstream task has trigger_rule=all_success, it will not run until all upstream tasks complete successfully.

If a previous task is skipped—for example, after conditional branching—and the next task has trigger_rule=all_success, it will also be skipped. To force execution even with skipped paths, use none_skipped or none_failed_or_skipped.

The Web interface visually displays the status of each task and clearly indicates if execution was blocked due to unmet trigger rules. This is useful for debugging the behavior of DAGs with multiple paths and optional tasks.

Additionally, the task log describes the reason for non-execution, based on unmet trigger rules.

Common Error Resolution

Task does not run even after upstream tasks complete
Check if the trigger_rule is compatible with previous outcomes.
The default all_success requires 100% success.

Task skipped without apparent reason
In DAGs with BranchPythonOperator, all tasks outside the
returned path are automatically skipped. Use dummy or adjust
the flow logic to avoid tasks being disregarded.

Cleanup task does not run after previous failure
Use trigger_rule='all_done' to ensure execution of final tasks
such as file cleanup or report sending.

Error referencing TriggerRule in code
Check if the TriggerRule module was correctly imported: from
airflow.utils.trigger_rule import TriggerRule.

Incomplete or incoherent execution flow
Review the logical chaining between tasks and validate each
task_id in the DAG graph. Flows with many branches may
require specific rules to consolidate final execution.

Best Practices

- Apply all_done for closing tasks that should always run

- Use one_failed for sending alerts only when needed

- Prefer none_failed_or_skipped in final tasks after
  branched flows

- Visually validate the flow in Graph View after configuring trigger rules

- Include explanatory comments in the code when using unconventional execution rules

Strategic Summary

Execution and dependency rules in Apache Airflow define the dynamic and resilient behavior of DAGs. Mastering the use of trigger rules allows the creation of smart pipelines, adaptable to multiple scenarios and capable of responding appropriately to failures, branches, and conditional completions. Correct configuration of these rules directly impacts the reliability of orchestration, preventing unnecessary executions or unexpected behaviors. With these practices established, workflows become more predictable, secure, and ready for critical operational environments.

CHAPTER 6. SCHEDULING AND EXECUTION INTERVALS

The control of DAG execution timing in Apache Airflow is handled through precise scheduling, defined using cron expressions or timedelta objects. Correctly defining these intervals is essential to ensure that workflows run at the expected time, without delays, duplications, or omissions. In addition, understanding the concepts of start_date, execution_date, backfill, and catchup helps avoid common misunderstandings about the real behavior of scheduled DAGs.

Cron and Timedelta

Airflow allows two main formats to define the execution interval of a DAG: cron expressions and timedelta.

The cron expression follows the UNIX standard with five fields:

python

```
schedule_interval = '0 6 * * *'  # Every day at 06:00
```

This configuration sets the DAG to run daily at 6 a.m. Other useful examples:

- '@daily': once per day

- '@hourly': every hour

- '0 0 * * 0': every Sunday at midnight

- '30 9 * * 1-5': at 09:30 Monday to Friday

You can also use timedelta objects for fixed intervals in seconds, minutes, hours, or days:

python

```
from datetime import timedelta


schedule_interval = timedelta(hours=2) # Runs every 2 hours
```

Airflow interprets these values as the interval between executions, not as an exact clock. Therefore, understanding the actual moment of execution requires attention to the use of start_date.

Start and End Times

The start_date field defines the exact instant from which the scheduler should begin considering executions for a DAG. This value must always be an explicit datetime with timezone, preferably UTC, to avoid ambiguity.

python

```
from datetime import datetime


start_date = datetime(2024, 1, 1, 0, 0) # Start of execution count
```

Airflow does not execute the DAG at the start_date. It treats this value as the reference moment to schedule the first execution, which will be based on the execution_date.

Additionally, you can define an end_date to limit the scheduling range. The DAG will be deactivated after this date.

python

```
end_date = datetime(2024, 12, 31)
```

Correctly defining start_date and schedule_interval avoids unexpected executions or multiple retroactive runs on the first load.

Start_date vs. Execution_date

This is one of the most important and often misunderstood concepts in Airflow. The start_date represents when the DAG should start being evaluated for execution. The execution_date is the date assigned to the DAG run, indicating the period being processed.

For example, a DAG with schedule_interval='@daily' and start_date=datetime(2024, 1, 1) will have its first run on January 2, with execution_date January 1. This happens because the DAG always runs after the period it represents.

This model is essential to ensure correct reprocessing of historical data and generate consistency in data warehouse pipelines.

Backfill and Catchup

Airflow allows DAGs to automatically run retroactive periods. This feature is called backfill, and its control is managed by the catchup parameter.

By default, catchup=True. This means that when a DAG is activated, Airflow will attempt to schedule runs for all periods between the start_date and the current date, respecting the schedule_interval.

Example: if a DAG with @daily was created with start_date=datetime(2024, 1, 1) and activated only on January 5, Airflow will attempt to run five runs with execution_dates from

January 1 to 5.

To disable this behavior:

python

catchup = False

With catchup=False, the DAG will run only from the moment it is activated, ignoring the history.
This configuration is recommended for DAGs that process real-time data or do not require reprocessing.

Common Error Resolution

DAG does not run on the expected date
Check that the start_date is not set to a future date relative to the system clock. Airflow only schedules DAGs with a start_date earlier than the current date.

Unexpected multiple executions when activating the DAG
This happens due to catchup=True. If you do not want retroactive runs, set catchup=False.

Confusion between execution_date and actual execution time
The execution_date represents the data period, not the time of execution. A DAG with execution_date=2024-01-01 will run on January 2.

Error using timedelta with invalid format
Always use the datetime.timedelta module to define custom intervals, avoiding values like strings or integers directly.

Off-time scheduling with poorly defined cron
Use online validation tools to confirm that the cron expression reflects the desired time. A common mistake is swapping minute and hour in the min hour day month day_of_week pattern.

Best Practices

- Define start_date clearly, always in the past and in UTC

- Use catchup=False for real-time DAGs or those that do not require reprocessing

- Prefer validated cron expressions for business hours, off-peak hours, or specific windows

- Avoid start_date=datetime.now() as it produces unpredictable behaviors

- Clearly document the scheduling impact on the business logic of the data

Strategic Summary

Scheduling and execution interval control in Apache Airflow is one of the pillars of correct pipeline operation. Clarity in defining schedule_interval, understanding the differences between start_date and execution_date, and consciously using catchup and backfill determine whether data will be processed at the right time and at the proper frequency. Mastering these concepts ensures operational reliability, orchestration predictability, and alignment with the business's processing windows. The next step in the journey involves deepening the use of XComs, the internal task communication mechanism.

CHAPTER 7. XCOMS: COMMUNICATION BETWEEN TASKS

XCom (cross-communication) is Apache Airflow's native mechanism for exchanging information between tasks within the same DAG. It allows a task to send temporary data to another, enabling a chained execution with the passing of values, intermediate results, and relevant metadata. While useful, using XComs requires well-defined technical criteria, as it involves data serialization and has a direct impact on Airflow's metadata database.

Introduction to Using XCom

XCom works on the idea that tasks can "push" and "pull" data from each other using a key-value structure. These records are stored in the application's metadata database and can be queried through Python code or the Web interface.

The purpose of XCom is to allow a task's results to be available to others, facilitating dynamic logic chaining without needing to rely on external cache systems or databases. It is a lightweight, fast mechanism integrated into the DAG's execution context.

xcom_push() and xcom_pull() Methods

The two main methods for working with XComs are xcom_push() and xcom_pull(). Both are accessible through the task context object (**context), automatically passed to PythonOperator functions via the provide_context=True parameter (in earlier versions) or directly via kwargs.

Example of using xcom_push():

python

```
def generate_value(**kwargs):
    kwargs['ti'].xcom_push(key='result', value=42)
```

This function inserts a value into XCom with the key 'result'. The ti parameter is the TaskInstance, representing the task's execution at that moment. This data can now be accessed by another task.

The task that will retrieve the value uses xcom_pull():

python

```
def use_value(**kwargs):
    value = kwargs['ti'].xcom_pull(task_ids='generate_value', key='result')
    print(f'The received value was: {value}')
```

The task_ids parameter indicates which task the value will be pulled from, and key specifies which key to retrieve. If the key is omitted, Airflow will attempt to pull the default value.

You can also use a Python function's return as an automatic push. When a function called by a PythonOperator returns something, that value is automatically stored in XCom with the key return_value.

python

```
def return_number():
    return 100
```

This value can be retrieved in the next task using:

python

```
value = kwargs['ti'].xcom_pull(task_ids='return_number')
```

Storing and Reading Temporary Data

XCom stores its data in the xcom table of the metadata database, with columns such as key, value, execution_date, and task_id. All values are serialized by default with the pickle module. Therefore, it's important that objects are simple and serializable, such as integers, strings, lists, or dictionaries.

Large or complex data can cause slowdowns, serialization errors, or impact database performance. The ideal use of XCom is for passing small structures that need to be consumed immediately by other tasks.

You can view records directly in the Web interface under the "XComs" menu of each DAG. This feature is useful for debugging task interactions and validating that data is being transferred correctly.

Risks and Precautions with Excessive Use

Although XCom is convenient, indiscriminate use can cause operational problems. Some main risks include:

- Excessive record buildup in the metadata database, impacting performance

- Serialization of incompatible objects, such as connections, files, or functions

- Task concurrency writing or reading the same keys

- Difficulty tracking in DAGs with multiple dependencies and ambiguous values

- Risk of leaking sensitive data if there's no control over stored content

Therefore, it's recommended to always name keys descriptively and uniquely, limit the size of the data, and avoid relying on XComs as the main integration layer between tasks.

In addition, tasks handling sensitive data should be cautious when storing any information in XCom records, as they can be accessed by administrators and are logged in the system.

Common Error Resolution

Serialization error when trying to save a complex object
Use only simple data types compatible with pickle. Avoid custom class objects or connections.

Returned value is None when using xcom_pull
Check if the upstream task ran successfully and if the specified key exists. It may be necessary to wait for the execution to finish.

Data not showing up in the Web interface
Only records generated by xcom_push() or return are displayed. Logs or prints do not affect XComs.

Key overwritten by multiple tasks
Ensure that task_ids and keys are unique per task. Avoid relying on the same key for multiple sources.

Error pulling value from a task that hasn't executed
Airflow does not automatically synchronize tasks. Make sure the dependency between tasks is correctly defined with >>.

Best Practices

- Use xcom_push() only for essential and transient data

- Prefer simple return values to pass results when possible

- Define the key explicitly and consistently to simplify reading and debugging

- Avoid large or sensitive objects in XCom values

- Limit XCom use to short-scope communication, not as an intermediate data store

Strategic Summary

XCom is a powerful and practical Airflow feature that allows tasks to share temporary data during DAG execution. When used correctly, it facilitates the creation of dynamic pipelines with conditional logic and smart stage coupling. However, excessive or improper use can compromise system performance, security, and predictability. Mastering xcom_push() and xcom_pull(), establishing good serialization practices, and maintaining discipline in DAG structure ensures efficient and secure communication between orchestrated tasks. Next, conditional flow with branching will be explored using the BranchPythonOperator.

CHAPTER 8. USING BRANCHING WITH BRANCHPYTHONOPERATOR

Branching is the feature that enables the conditional execution of different paths in a DAG, based on programmatic decisions defined at runtime. In Apache Airflow, the operator responsible for this functionality is the BranchPythonOperator, which acts as a logical switch within the pipeline, deciding which task(s) should be executed next according to criteria defined by the developer. This approach is essential for creating dynamic, adaptable workflows with granular control over business logic.

Conditional Task Execution

In a traditional linear DAG, all tasks are executed in sequence or in parallel, according to the defined dependencies. When there's a need to follow different paths based on conditions, branching comes into play. The conditional logic is written in a Python function, which returns one or more task_ids of the tasks that should be executed after the decision.

This type of structure is common in pipelines involving multiple data sources, different processing types, context validations, or alternative execution strategies.

Returning Valid Task Names

The function assigned to the BranchPythonOperator must return a string with the task_id of the next task to be executed, or a list of strings if more than one task is to be activated simultaneously. Tasks that are not chosen are automatically marked as skipped by the scheduler and will not be executed unless there's a custom trigger_rule.

Simple example with a single task return:

python

```python
def choose_task():
    condition = check_parameters()
    if condition:
        return 'task_a'
    return 'task_b'
```

For multiple tasks:

python

```python
def multiple_destinations():
    return ['task_1', 'task_2']
```

These task_ids must exactly match the identifiers of the tasks declared in the DAG. Any typos or inconsistencies will prevent execution and result in silent failures or unpredictable behavior.

Implementing Logical Paths

Practical implementation starts with defining the branching operator. The BranchPythonOperator is configured with the standard parameters, plus python_callable, which should point to the decision function.

python

```python
from airflow.operators.python import BranchPythonOperator

branch = BranchPythonOperator(
```

```
    task_id='choose_path',

    python_callable=choose_task,

    dag=dag

)
```

Next, the alternative paths are defined:

python

```
task_a = PythonOperator(

    task_id='task_a',

    python_callable=execute_a,

    dag=dag

)


task_b = PythonOperator(

    task_id='task_b',

    python_callable=execute_b,

    dag=dag

)
```

The chaining should be clearly established, linking the branch operator to the tasks that may be chosen:

python

```
branch >> [task_a, task_b]
```

In many cases, it's necessary to consolidate the flows at a

common point after branching. Since skipped tasks block the execution of subsequent tasks with trigger_rule=all_success, it's mandatory to use trigger_rule=one_success or none_failed_or_skipped for the joining task.

python

```
final = PythonOperator(
    task_id='final_task',
    python_callable=finish,
    trigger_rule='none_failed_or_skipped',
    dag=dag
)


[task_a, task_b] >> final
```

Example with Multiple Alternative Flows

Consider a validation pipeline that must execute different paths for Brazilian customers and customers from other countries. The conditional logic checks the country code and sets the task to execute.

python

```
def decide_country(**kwargs):
    country = kwargs['dag_run'].conf.get('country', 'BR')
    if country == 'BR':
        return 'process_brazil'
    return 'process_foreign'
```

Branch operator:

python

```
branch = BranchPythonOperator(
    task_id='define_route',
    python_callable=decide_country,
    provide_context=True,
    dag=dag
)
```

Conditional tasks:

python

```
br = PythonOperator(
    task_id='process_brazil',
    python_callable=process_br,
    dag=dag
)
```

```
foreign = PythonOperator(
    task_id='process_foreign',
    python_callable=process_others,
    dag=dag
)
```

Flow consolidation:

python

```
final = PythonOperator(
```

```
    task_id='finalize_pipeline',

    python_callable=close,

    trigger_rule='none_failed_or_skipped',

    dag=dag

)
```

branch >> [br, foreign] >> final

This model allows the DAG to select the appropriate path based on parameters provided externally via API, interface, or manual configuration at trigger time.

Common Error Resolution

Expected task does not run after BranchPythonOperator
Ensure that the task_id returned by the conditional function is correctly spelled and matches the declared task.

Consolidation task does not run after branching
Use trigger_rule='none_failed_or_skipped' to allow the task to execute even when one of the upstream tasks is skipped.

Context error in the decision function
Ensure that provide_context=True is set or that **kwargs is used correctly in the function signature.

Unexpected behavior in DAGs with multiple branching levels
Review the logic and check for overlapping task_ids, loops, or circular dependencies. Organize visually in Graph View.

Incorrect skips propagating through the DAG
Avoid setting trigger_rule=all_success on tasks following multiple alternative paths. Prefer permissive rules for reconnection points.

Best Practices

- Use descriptive and unique names for each execution path

- Logically validate all possible conditions within the conditional function

- End branched paths with a common point using the appropriate trigger_rule

- Limit branching complexity to one level per DAG whenever possible

- Avoid ambiguous conditional logic or logic based on volatile data outside the DAG

Strategic Summary

The use of BranchPythonOperator in Airflow provides decision-making power within DAGs, allowing different flows to run based on business logic, input parameters, or contextual conditions. This branching capability gives pipelines an additional layer of operational intelligence, adaptability, and modularity. When well-structured, branching transforms static DAGs into responsive, rule-driven systems without compromising traceability or execution control. Mastering this technique is fundamental for modern data orchestration architectures.

CHAPTER 9. SENSORS: MONITORING EXTERNAL CONDITIONS

Sensors are specialized operators in Apache Airflow designed to wait for the occurrence of an external event before allowing the continuation of an execution flow. They function as active or passive waiting mechanisms, monitoring conditions outside the DAG and releasing the sequence of tasks only when the defined criterion is met. This functionality is critical in pipelines that depend on files, APIs, third-party data, or tasks executed in other DAGs.

Unlike regular operators, Sensors do not perform a direct productive action. Their sole purpose is to observe. Proper use of this tool promotes system synchronization, reduces failures in dependent tasks, and allows greater flexibility when integrating heterogeneous flows. However, misuse can cause serious performance bottlenecks, resource locking, and worker saturation.

What They Are and How They Work

In practice, a Sensor is a type of operator that extends the BaseSensorOperator class. The main difference is that it repeatedly performs a check—usually within a loop—until the desired external event is detected or the user-defined timeout is reached.

The Sensor logic is simple:

- Check if the condition is met

- If yes, finish successfully

- If no, wait for the poke_interval and try again

- If the total time exceeds timeout, finish with failure

Sensors can operate in two distinct modes: poke and reschedule. In the default poke mode, the worker remains allocated while waiting for the condition. In reschedule mode, the Sensor releases the worker between attempts, making the system more scalable.

These operators are often used in pipelines that process files delivered by other systems, wait for a response from an external endpoint, or depend on the prior execution of another DAG.

FileSensor, HttpSensor, ExternalTaskSensor

Airflow offers a variety of ready-to-use sensors. The most common are FileSensor, HttpSensor, and ExternalTaskSensor.

FileSensor

Monitors the existence of a file or directory. It's ideal for workflows that wait for the arrival of a CSV, JSON, spreadsheet, or any other externally generated artifact.

python

```
from airflow.sensors.filesystem import FileSensor


wait_for_file = FileSensor(
    task_id='check_file',
    filepath='/data/input.csv',
    poke_interval=30,
    timeout=600,
```

```
    mode='poke',

    dag=dag

)
```

- filepath: path of the file to monitor

- poke_interval: interval between verification attempts (in seconds)

- timeout: maximum waiting time before marking as failure

HttpSensor

Checks the availability of an HTTP endpoint. Useful for checking if an API is online, if a service has started correctly, or if a URL is accessible.

python

```
from airflow.sensors.http_sensor import HttpSensor


check_api = HttpSensor(

    task_id='check_api',

    http_conn_id='external_api',

    endpoint='/status',

    poke_interval=20,

    timeout=300,

    mode='reschedule',

    dag=dag

)
```

The http_conn_id must be preconfigured in Airflow connections. The sensor checks the response status and can be customized to validate the returned content.

ExternalTaskSensor

Tracks the execution of a specific task in another DAG. This sensor is essential to synchronize dependencies between separate pipelines.

python

```python
from airflow.sensors.external_task import ExternalTaskSensor


wait_for_external_dag = ExternalTaskSensor(
    task_id='wait_for_previous_pipeline',
    external_dag_id='data_input_dag',
    external_task_id='validate_data',
    allowed_states=['success'],
    failed_states=['failed', 'skipped'],
    mode='poke',
    timeout=900,
    dag=dag
)
```

This sensor checks the status of the validate_data task in the data_input_dag DAG and only releases execution if it completes successfully.

Configuration of Retries, Timeout, and Wait Mode

Every Sensor can be configured with parameters that control its behavior. The most important are:

- poke_interval: defines the interval between each condition check. A very low value consumes more resources; a high value may delay the DAG.

- timeout: specifies the total time allowed for the Sensor to wait. After this period, the task is marked as failed.

- mode: determines the operation mode. It can be poke (default) or reschedule. The reschedule mode is preferred in environments with multiple DAGs and limited workers.

- retries: number of retry attempts after failure.

- retry_delay: waiting time between attempts after a failure.

Example of robust configuration:

python

```python
sensor_custom = FileSensor(
    task_id='wait_for_report',
    filepath='/reports/daily.csv',
    poke_interval=60,
    timeout=1800,
    mode='reschedule',
    retries=2,
    retry_delay=timedelta(minutes=5),
    dag=dag
)
```

This configuration allows a sensor to wait up to 30 minutes for the file, checking every 60 seconds, and retrying up to two times, waiting five minutes between attempts if it fails.

Performance and Impact on Workers

Improper use of Sensors can cause scalability issues in Airflow. When used in poke mode, each Sensor consumes a dedicated worker while waiting for the condition to be met. In environments with few workers and many concurrent DAGs, this can quickly exhaust system resources, causing queues, slowdowns, and timeout failures.

To mitigate this risk, reschedule mode should be used whenever possible. In this mode, the Sensor is suspended and taken off the queue between attempts, freeing the worker for other tasks. This is especially important in pipelines that monitor conditions with long waiting periods.

In addition, very low poke_interval values increase the number of accesses and checks, which can overload monitored services, network files, or external databases.

Indiscriminate use of ExternalTaskSensors in poke mode for DAGs with multiple cross-dependencies should also be avoided, as it can create a domino effect of chained resource consumption.

Common Error Resolution

Sensor fails even when the condition is met
Check if the path, endpoint, or external identifier is correct. Also, validate if the condition was truly satisfied at the time of execution.

Sensor never finishes execution
It may be that the condition is not being satisfied and the

timeout is too high. Use a larger poke_interval and limit the timeout to avoid blocked DAGs.

Worker stays busy indefinitely
Sensors in poke mode retain the worker. Switch to mode='reschedule' for long waits.

Error monitoring external DAG
Check if the DAG name and task name are correct. The external_task_id must exist and be running.

API responds with 403 or 500 error
The HttpSensor only considers HTTP 200 as success. Adjust the content checking function or review the connection authentication.

Best Practices

- Use mode='reschedule' for sensors waiting long periods

- Define a reasonable timeout to avoid DAGs blocked for hours

- Monitor the number of tasks in prolonged execution in the Web UI

- Clearly document each Sensor's function to ease maintenance

- Centralize poke_interval and timeout values in variables for standardization

Strategic Summary

Sensors in Apache Airflow provide a critical control layer to synchronize pipelines with external events, ensuring execution occurs only when specific conditions are met. When well configured, they enable the construction of robust, responsive, and externally integrated workflows. The correct choice of operation modes, timing adjustments, and clear dependency definitions are essential to maintain the balance between reliability and performance. Mastering sensors distinguishes static operational pipelines from intelligent, ecosystem-aware flows. The next stage in learning focuses on direct monitoring of DAGs and tasks through logs and dashboards, consolidating operational visibility of the environment.

CHAPTER 10. MONITORING DAGS AND TASKS

Efficient monitoring of DAGs and tasks in Apache Airflow is fundamental to ensuring the reliability, traceability, and robustness of data pipelines. Having complete visibility over the execution state of DAGs, the logs generated by each task, the execution history, and system metrics is a mandatory requirement in production environments. Without a well-configured observability system, silent failures, delays, or unexpected behaviors can go unnoticed, directly impacting data flows, analyses, and business decisions.

Airflow natively offers a powerful web interface that allows real-time tracking of DAG execution. In addition, it can be integrated with external observability tools like Grafana, Prometheus, Elasticsearch, and others, allowing the creation of customized dashboards and continuous monitoring with alerts and historical analyses. Mastery of this monitoring layer enables proactive action, precise problem diagnosis, and SLA assurance in critical pipelines.

Logs and Interpretation of Results

Each task executed in a DAG generates detailed logs, recording everything from environment setup to process completion, with return codes, error messages, execution time, and context variables. Logs are the primary source of information for diagnosing and validating DAG behavior.

By default, logs are stored in the local file system in a structure organized by DAG, task, and execution date:

php

```
~/airflow/logs/<dag_id>/<task_id>/<execution_date>/
```

When accessing the Airflow web interface, the user can click the "Log" button next to each task run to view this content. Logs are divided into stages and usually include:

- Task initialization and context loading

- Operator and module imports

- Task code execution (with print or logging output)

- Final status: success, failure, or error

- Full traceback in case of exceptions

These details help identify:

- Syntax errors or module import failures

- Connection failures with databases, APIs, or external systems

- Undefined or missing variables

- Timeout, permission, and encoding issues

It is always recommended to use logging.info(), logging.warning(), and logging.error() instead of print(), as these methods provide better control, standardization, and integration with external logging systems.

Example of correct use of the logging module:

python

```
import logging

def execute_task():
    logging.info("Starting processing task")
    result = process_data()
    logging.info(f"Final result: {result}")
```

With this, logs will have timestamps and severity levels that facilitate analysis.

Besides access via the interface, logs can be exported to services like Amazon S3, Google Cloud Storage, or enterprise logging systems like ELK Stack, allowing long-term retention, advanced searches, and consolidation of logs from multiple DAGs.

Dashboard and Metrics Visualization

The Airflow Web UI is the main native monitoring interface. The homepage lists all registered DAGs with status, last run time, and quick action buttons such as manual trigger, pause, and graph view.

Clicking on a specific DAG provides several visualizations:

- **Tree View**: displays a timeline map of DAG executions, with color coding by status (green for success, red for failure, gray for skipped)

- **Graph View**: shows the DAG's dependency graph, useful for understanding the structure and chaining

- **Gantt View**: visualizes the duration of each task on a timeline, helping identify bottlenecks and slow stages

- **Task Duration**: chart with historical task duration over time

- **Landing Times**: shows the difference between the scheduled and actual execution times of each DAG run

These views help identify:

- Which tasks are causing DAG delays

- Whether there is imbalance in parallel task execution

- The average execution time per task

- When failures or slowdowns begin to occur

Additionally, under the "Browse > DAG Runs" or "Browse > Task Instances" menus, you can get a complete table with all executions, statuses, dates, duration, and actions for each DAG and task instance.

Use of External Tools (Grafana, Prometheus)

For more advanced environments with multiple pipelines and strict SLAs, it is recommended to integrate Airflow with external observability tools. The most commonly used are Grafana and Prometheus, which allow real-time monitoring, automatic alert generation, and consolidated visualization of operational metrics.

Prometheus can connect to Airflow through the official Exporter or using custom APIs. It collects metrics such as:

- Number of active DAGs

- Average execution time per DAG

- Number of failures over time

- Worker utilization

- Tasks in "queued," "running," "failed" states

These metrics are then exposed via the /metrics endpoint and consumed by Prometheus, which stores the data and enables advanced queries with PromQL.

Grafana acts as the visual frontend for these metrics. It's possible to create dashboards with line charts, bars, status panels, and visual alerts. Recommended panels include:

- Executions per hour, day, or week

- DAGs with the highest failure rates

- Tasks with the highest average execution time

- Execution history of critical tasks

- Heatmap of running DAGs by time of day

This enables trend visualization, anomaly detection, and bottleneck prediction in the system. These tools can also be integrated with alert systems like PagerDuty, Slack, Microsoft Teams, or email, allowing automated incident responses.

Failure Diagnosis with Detailed Logs

When a DAG or task fails, diagnosis starts with analyzing the generated logs. By default, Airflow provides clear messages about the source of the error, including:

- Name of the module or operator that caused the exception

- Exact line of the error in the Python code

- Complete exception traceback

- Variable values at runtime

- Custom messages generated by logging.error() or logging.exception()

These details are usually sufficient to resolve most operational issues, from typos to connection failures with external systems.

In more complex cases, such as intermittent failures, it is necessary to analyze the occurrence pattern over time. Tools like Grafana help identify if the error is related to:

- Specific data loads

- System peak times

- Recent changes in the DAG or input data

- Infrastructure problems, such as full disk or memory shortage

It is also possible to configure failure callbacks (on_failure_callback) so that, upon detecting a failure, Airflow sends automatic alerts, logs the error to external systems, or even runs automatic correction scripts.

Common Error Resolution

DAG does not appear in the interface
Check if the DAG Python file is correctly saved in the dags/ directory, without syntax errors, and if the dag_id is unique.

Task runs but does not generate a log
Ensure the operator is generating output with logging and that

the log path is accessible. Check file system permissions.

Generic error without traceback
Enable log_level = DEBUG in airflow.cfg for more detailed messages. Make sure the DAG is in debug mode if necessary.

Metrics do not appear in Prometheus
Validate if the Exporter is correctly installed and accessible on the expected port. Check if scraping is enabled in Prometheus and if the DAG names are correct.

Grafana panel shows no data
Check if the panel is pointing to the correct data source and if the PromQL queries are returning values. Use recent dates and review the time range.

Best Practices

- Use logging instead of print() to generate standardized technical logs

- Monitor critical DAGs with customized Grafana dashboards

- Set up automatic alerts based on repeated failures or slow executions

- Standardize log messages with context prefixes to facilitate searches

- Rotate old logs to avoid excessive disk usage

Strategic Summary

Monitoring DAGs and tasks in Apache Airflow is an essential pillar for the safe and efficient operation of data pipelines.

The combination of the native interface, detailed logs, and integrations with observability systems like Grafana and Prometheus provides full visibility into flow behavior. Quickly diagnosing failures, precisely identifying bottlenecks, and anticipating problems through alerts are mandatory capabilities in production environments. With consistent logging practices, metric configuration, and analysis structure, Airflow becomes a complete, transparent orchestration platform ready to scale in mission-critical scenarios.

CHAPTER 11. CUSTOMIZING OPERATORS AND HOOKS

Apache Airflow stands out as an extensible platform, allowing developers to create custom components to adapt the tool's behavior to the specific needs of their ecosystem. The ability to customize operators and hooks offers an essential layer of flexibility to connect Airflow to legacy systems, unsupported APIs, proprietary data flows, and complex automation strategies.

Custom operators encapsulate specific task logic, while custom hooks allow the establishment of reusable connections and abstractions with external services. By building these tailored components, it's possible to standardize interactions, reduce redundancies, and increase code cohesion across DAGs. This chapter presents, in depth, how to create, structure, and maintain custom operators and hooks in Airflow, focusing on reuse, testing, clarity, and scalability.

Creating New Operators

Custom operators are created by inheriting from the BaseOperator class or from an existing operator. They must implement the execute() method, where the task logic will be performed. The creation process starts with defining the parameters the operator will accept, usually through the __init__() method, and implementing the operational logic in execute().

Basic structure of a custom operator:

python

```python
from airflow.models import BaseOperator
from airflow.utils.context import Context
import logging


class MyCustomOperator(BaseOperator):
    def __init__(self, parameter_1, parameter_2, **kwargs):
        super().__init__(**kwargs)
        self.parameter_1 = parameter_1
        self.parameter_2 = parameter_2

    def execute(self, context: Context):
        logging.info(f"Executing operator with {self.parameter_1} and {self.parameter_2}")
        result = self.parameter_1 + self.parameter_2
        logging.info(f"Result: {result}")
```

After creation, this operator can be imported normally into any DAG and used as a task:

python

```python
task = MyCustomOperator(
    task_id='run_custom',
    parameter_1=10,
    parameter_2=20,
    dag=dag
```

)

It's crucial to keep the operator in a separate directory (plugins/), properly versioned and tested. It's also recommended to write a clear docstring explaining the parameters, behavior, and requirements.

Custom operators are useful for encapsulating routines that would frequently be repeated across multiple DAGs, such as schema validation, processing proprietary formatted files, integration with internal systems, or automation orchestration.

Implementing Custom Hooks

Hooks are classes that extend BaseHook and encapsulate the logic for connecting and communicating with data sources or external APIs. While operators represent tasks, hooks are responsible for providing reusable methods for external interactions, such as sending requests, running queries, reading remote files, and more.

Example of a custom hook to connect to a reports API:

python

```python
from airflow.hooks.base import BaseHook
import requests


class ReportAPIHook(BaseHook):
    def __init__(self, conn_id='report_api'):
        self.conn_id = conn_id
        self.base_url = self.get_connection(conn_id).host
        self.token = self.get_connection(conn_id).password
```

```python
def fetch_data(self, endpoint):
    headers = {'Authorization': f'Bearer {self.token}'}
    url = f'{self.base_url}/{endpoint}'
    response = requests.get(url, headers=headers)
    response.raise_for_status()
    return response.json()
```

To use this hook inside an operator or PythonOperator:

python
```python
def task():
    hook = ReportAPIHook()
    data = hook.fetch_data('reports/daily')
    print(data)
```

Hooks can be completely decoupled from operators and maintained as internal libraries for use in multiple contexts. This promotes reuse and centralization of integration logic, simplifying maintenance and testing.

Inheritance Structure and Logic Reuse

The creation of custom operators and hooks should always follow the principle of reuse. Instead of duplicating code across multiple classes, it's best to build a modular and hierarchical structure using inheritance and composition.

A good example is creating a base class with common functions and deriving specific operators from it:

python

```python
class BaseOperatorTemplate(BaseOperator):
    def log_start(self):
        logging.info("Starting execution...")


    def log_end(self):
        logging.info("Ending execution.")
```

Derived operator:

python

```python
class FinanceOperator(BaseOperatorTemplate):
    def __init__(self, account_id, **kwargs):
        super().__init__(**kwargs)
        self.account_id = account_id


    def execute(self, context):
        self.log_start()
        self.process_account(self.account_id)
        self.log_end()


    def process_account(self, id):
        # processing logic
        pass
```

This pattern facilitates mass updates, ensures consistency among operators in the same family, and reduces implementation errors. The same concept applies to hooks, where utility functions for requests, error handling, or authentication can be isolated in superclasses.

Deploying Reusable Components

For custom operators and hooks to be used throughout the Airflow environment, they must be made accessible and organized. The main deployment approaches include:

- plugins/ directory: default location for custom components. Saving operators and hooks here allows Airflow to recognize them automatically.

- Python packages: encapsulate components in a versioned Python package and install it via pip in Airflow's virtual environment. Ideal for environments with multiple developers.

- Git repositories: use Git submodules to integrate shared component repositories into each project's DAGs.

- Docker containers: include the custom operator and hook files in the Airflow Docker image, ensuring portability and consistency across environments.

Additionally, maintain a naming convention and directory structure that allows components to be quickly located. The following organization is suggested:

```
plugins/
├── operators/
│   ├── finance_operator.py
│   ├── email_operator.py
├── hooks/
```

```
|    ├── sap_hook.py
|    ├── s3_custom_hook.py
```

It's also recommended to include an __init__.py file in each folder to enable direct importing.

Common Error Resolution

Operator not recognized by DAG
Check if the operator file is in the plugins/ directory and if it's being imported correctly into the DAG. Ensure the class name is consistent.

Circular import error
Avoid importing DAGs inside operators or hooks themselves. The architecture should be one-directional: hooks are used by operators, operators are used by DAGs.

Failure to access connection in the hook
Make sure the connection is properly registered in the Web interface and that conn_id exactly matches what's defined in the hook.

Serialization issues when using complex objects as parameters
Use only simple types like strings, integers, and lists as operator parameters. Avoid passing objects like custom class instances directly.

Hook does not return data or fails silently
Implement robust exception handling with try/except and log clear messages with logging.error() to aid in diagnosis.

Best Practices

- Document operators and hooks with clear docstrings and usage examples

- Standardize names with Operator and Hook suffixes for easy identification

- Isolate integration logic in hooks and keep operators focused on flow control

- Use structured logging at all execution points

- Write unit tests for operators and hooks, ensuring minimum coverage

- Reuse common logic through inheritance and helper classes

- Avoid hardcoding: always use parameters and variables when possible

Strategic Summary

Creating custom operators and hooks in Apache Airflow is a powerful strategy to adapt the tool to an organization's specific needs. These components promote standardization, encapsulation, and reuse, making pipelines more robust, readable, and sustainable. Hooks enable centralized integration with any external system, while operators organize the execution logic of specialized tasks.

CHAPTER 12. PARALLELISM AND CONCURRENCY

The scalability of Apache Airflow is directly tied to its ability to execute simultaneous tasks across multiple workers, efficiently distributing workload. To achieve this level of performance, it's necessary to understand and correctly configure parallelism and concurrency parameters, ensuring that infrastructure resources are optimally used without overload or idleness.

The concepts of parallelism, concurrency, dag_concurrency, max_active_runs, and pools form the foundation of concurrent execution control in Airflow. Each of these parameters directly impacts how many tasks can run at the same time—globally, per DAG, per worker, or per task type.

Understanding these limits, combined with best practices in partitioning and execution planning, enables the creation of robust, fast, and scalable data pipelines. This chapter explores each of these concepts in depth, explains how to configure them properly, and guides how to diagnose execution bottlenecks or blockages.

Simultaneous Workers

Task execution in Airflow is handled by processes called workers, which receive scheduled tasks from the scheduler and execute the code associated with each operator. The number of available workers and how they scale depends on the configured executor type:

- SequentialExecutor: runs one task at a time; used only for testing and local environments.

- LocalExecutor: allows multiple simultaneous tasks on the same server.

- CeleryExecutor: distributes tasks across multiple workers on different machines.

- KubernetesExecutor: runs each task in an isolated pod, offering maximum scalability.

In production environments, using CeleryExecutor or KubernetesExecutor is highly recommended, as they allow true parallel execution with fault tolerance and load balancing. Each worker can process multiple simultaneous tasks, depending on the worker_concurrency setting.

Example configuration in airflow.cfg:

ini

[celery]

worker_concurrency = 16

This value defines how many tasks each worker can execute simultaneously. If there are two workers, the total possible will be 32 parallel tasks, depending on the machine's hardware capacity.

Configuration of parallelism,

concurrency, **and** dag_concurrency

Parallelism behavior in Airflow is controlled by several parameters in airflow.cfg:

- parallelism: the maximum number of tasks that can run simultaneously across all of Airflow (global limit).

- dag_concurrency: the maximum number of active tasks simultaneously in a single DAG.

- max_active_runs_per_dag: the maximum number of DAG instances that can run simultaneously.

- task_concurrency: an optional parameter defined directly on the DAG object to limit concurrency for a specific task.

These values should be adjusted according to data volume, pipeline architecture, and available resources.

Example configuration in airflow.cfg:

ini

```ini
[core]
parallelism = 128
dag_concurrency = 32
```

Example in the DAG code:

python

```python
from airflow import DAG

dag = DAG(
    dag_id='monthly_processing',
    schedule_interval='@daily',
    max_active_runs=3,
    concurrency=10
)
```

This DAG will allow at most three instances to run in parallel, with up to 10 simultaneous tasks per instance.

Execution Limits and Performance Best Practices

Execution parameter configuration should always consider:

- Actual environment capacity: number of CPUs, RAM, and bandwidth.

- Type of executed tasks: lightweight tasks like file copies consume little, but heavy processing or API calls may require stricter limits.

- Time sensitivity: critical DAGs should have priority over low-frequency DAGs.

Performance best practices include:

- Using asynchronous operators whenever possible (e.g., AsyncHttpOperator)

- Avoiding mass use of poke sensors; prefer reschedule mode

- Distributing heavy tasks into separate DAGs or alternate schedules

- Prioritizing DAGs and tasks with priority_weight

- Reducing each task's execution time to improve parallelism

- Consolidating short tasks into larger batches to reduce overhead

It's crucial to monitor performance via the web interface and logs, watching for tasks stuck in queued state, which may indicate resource or configuration bottlenecks.

Using Pools for Fine-Grained Control

Pools are an advanced execution control tool in Airflow, allowing you to limit how many tasks of a certain type or group can run simultaneously. Each task can be assigned to a pool, and Airflow ensures that the maximum number of active tasks in that group never exceeds the limit.

This is useful for controlling concurrent access to:

- External APIs with request limits

- Databases with high connection costs

- Third-party services with usage billing

- Heavy processes that should not saturate the server

Pools are created through the web interface (Admin > Pools) or via CLI:

bash

```
airflow pools set report_api_pool 5 "Pool for report API"
```

In the operator, simply indicate the desired pool:

python

```
task = PythonOperator(
    task_id='call_api',
    python_callable=call_endpoint,
    pool='api_pool',
```

```
    dag=dag
)
```

If the number of simultaneous tasks reaches the pool limit, new executions will remain queued until slots are available.

Pools also help ensure that priority DAGs have preferential resource access when combined with priority_weight.

Common Error Resolution

Tasks remain indefinitely in queued
Check if the parallelism or dag_concurrency values are too low. Confirm that workers are available and active in the environment.

Too much concurrent execution freezes the system
Reduce worker_concurrency and adjust max_active_runs_per_dag to prevent excessive parallelism in heavy DAGs.

Task fails with pool error
Confirm that the specified pool exists and that slots are available. Adjust the maximum number of slots or create multiple pools.

Increased queue time between tasks
This may indicate a worker limit or blockage in specific DAGs. Use Gantt View to identify tasks delaying the queue.

DAGs ignore configured execution limits
Check if concurrency and max_active_runs are correctly configured in the DAG definition and in airflow.cfg.

Best Practices

- Adjust parallelism and dag_concurrency according to environment load

- Use max_active_runs_per_dag to prevent simultaneous execution overload

- Create pools for critical tasks or those that consume external APIs

- Monitor workers with dashboards and queue metrics

- Prioritize tasks and DAGs with priority_weight in Celery environments

- Validate behavior with test DAGs before applying in production

- Separate DAGs by workload type: batch, streaming, alerts

- Define SLAs to identify bottlenecks and prevent tasks from exceeding execution windows

Strategic Summary

Managing parallelism and concurrency is one of the pillars of performance in Apache Airflow. Understanding and correctly configuring execution parameters allows you to scale the system without compromising stability. Simultaneous workers, parallelism values, concurrency, use of pools, and constant analysis of queues and active executions are tools that enable the operation of complex pipelines safely and predictably. Applying best practices and continuous monitoring ensures that each DAG uses only the necessary resources, maintaining the overall environment balance.

CHAPTER 13. PRODUCTION DEPLOYMENT WITH DOCKER

Apache Airflow, as a modular and distributed platform, finds one of its most effective production deployment solutions in Docker. Using containers ensures portability, configuration consistency, dependency isolation, and easy environment replication. By packaging Airflow into Docker images, you can precisely control all its dependencies, components, and interactions with the operating system, regardless of the underlying infrastructure.

This section presents a practical and objective guide to deploying a fully functional Airflow instance using Docker, including image building, defining persistent volumes, configuring environment variables, using Docker Compose, and scalability strategies for production. The approach is guided by principles of operational robustness, simplified maintenance, and adaptation to multiple usage scenarios.

Configuring Docker Image for Airflow

The official Apache Airflow project already provides a Docker image maintained by the community and regularly updated with support for various executors, operators, and extras. The base image is hosted on Docker Hub under the name:

bash

```
apache/airflow:<tag>
```

The correct tag selection depends on the desired version and executor used. Example:

bash

```
apache/airflow:2.7.2-python3.9
```

For customized environments, it's common to create a custom image extending the official one. This allows adding dependencies, plugins, DAGs, or specific configurations.

Example Dockerfile:

dockerfile

```
FROM apache/airflow:2.7.2-python3.9


USER root
RUN apt-get update && apt-get install -y gcc


USER airflow
COPY requirements.txt .
RUN pip install --no-cache-dir -r requirements.txt


COPY dags/ /opt/airflow/dags/
COPY plugins/ /opt/airflow/plugins/
```

This Dockerfile adds system packages, installs specific Python dependencies, and incorporates custom DAGs and plugins. The image can be built with:

bash

```
docker build -t airflow-production:latest .
```

Volumes, Environment Variables, and Scheduler Container

A functional Airflow architecture requires defining multiple services: webserver, scheduler, worker (in some cases), triggerer, flower (Celery monitoring), and the metadata database (PostgreSQL or MySQL). All these services share a common code base and need volumes to maintain persistent data.

Common volumes include:

- /opt/airflow/dags: DAG code

- /opt/airflow/logs: execution logs

- /opt/airflow/plugins: custom plugins

- /root/.aws: AWS credentials (if necessary)

Example mounting in docker-compose.yml:

yaml

```
volumes:
  - ./dags:/opt/airflow/dags
  - ./logs:/opt/airflow/logs
  - ./plugins:/opt/airflow/plugins
```

Environment variables are defined in the environment block or in .env files, controlling everything from database connections to execution policies.

Example variables:

yaml

```
AIRFLOW__CORE__EXECUTOR: LocalExecutor
AIRFLOW__DATABASE__SQL_ALCHEMY_CONN: postgresql+psycopg2://airflow:airflow@postgres/airflow
AIRFLOW__CORE__FERNET_KEY: 'generatedfernetkey123...'
AIRFLOW__CORE__LOAD_EXAMPLES: 'False'
```

The scheduler is one of the required services and must run in the background, coordinating DAG execution based on schedules and dependencies. It's defined as an independent container in Compose.

Docker Compose and Local Environment Replication

The docker-compose.yml file is the most practical and standardized way to organize the containers needed to run Airflow in any environment. The official project provides a repository with a complete working template that can be adapted as needed.

Simplified docker-compose.yml example:

yaml

```
version: '3'
services:
  postgres:
    image: postgres:13
    environment:
      POSTGRES_USER: airflow
      POSTGRES_PASSWORD: airflow
      POSTGRES_DB: airflow
```

```yaml
    volumes:
      - postgres-db-volume:/var/lib/postgresql/data

  airflow-webserver:
    image: airflow-production:latest
    depends_on:
      - postgres
    environment:
      - AIRFLOW__CORE__EXECUTOR=LocalExecutor
    volumes:
      - ./dags:/opt/airflow/dags
      - ./logs:/opt/airflow/logs
    ports:
      - "8080:8080"
    command: webserver

  airflow-scheduler:
    image: airflow-production:latest
    depends_on:
      - airflow-webserver
    volumes:
      - ./dags:/opt/airflow/dags
      - ./logs:/opt/airflow/logs
    command: scheduler
```

```
volumes:
  postgres-db-volume:
```

To initialize the environment, simply run:

bash

```
docker-compose up airflow-init
docker-compose up -d
```

This model allows local environment replication to any server with Docker installed, maintaining configuration consistency and reducing setup time in new environments.

Cluster Scalability

Airflow scalability with Docker depends on the executor used:

- LocalExecutor: allows local parallelism, but limited to server capacity.

- CeleryExecutor: distributes tasks across multiple workers in separate containers.

- KubernetesExecutor: creates an isolated pod per task, with near-infinite scalability in Kubernetes clusters.

To scale with Celery, simply start multiple containers with the worker command:

yaml

```
airflow-worker:
  image: airflow-production:latest
```

```yaml
depends_on:
  - postgres
environment:
  - AIRFLOW__CORE__EXECUTOR=CeleryExecutor
command: worker
```

The task queue is orchestrated by a broker (Redis or RabbitMQ), which must also be configured as a service:

yaml

```yaml
redis:
  image: redis:6
  ports:
    - "6379:6379"
```

With this model, you can dynamically add or remove workers with:

bash

```bash
docker-compose up -d --scale airflow-worker=4
```

For large-scale production environments, it's recommended to move the infrastructure to a Kubernetes cluster using KubernetesExecutor or the official Airflow Helm Chart. This approach offers native autoscaling, centralized secret management, advanced observability, and complete execution isolation.

Common Error Resolution

Webserver fails to initialize
Check if the airflow db init command was run before bringing up the containers. Ensure that database variables are correct.

Permission error in volumes
Ensure that the dags/, logs/, and plugins/ directories have permissions compatible with the airflow user inside the container.

Scheduler running but tasks not firing
This may be due to a misconfigured executor or missing worker. Confirm that the executor in AIRFLOW__CORE__EXECUTOR matches the defined services.

Workers not receiving tasks
If using Celery, check the Redis broker connection. The issue may be in AIRFLOW__CELERY__BROKER_URL or the service startup.

Connection refused at http://localhost:8080
The port mapping may be missing in docker-compose.yml. Ensure the webserver service has ports: - "8080:8080" defined.

Best Practices

- Use official images as base, with minimal extension for compatibility

- Control dependencies with requirements.txt and automated build

- Version docker-compose.yml files to ensure reproducibility

- Use .env to keep secrets and environment variables out of the code

- Separate staging and production environments with specific configs

- Automate initialization with entrypoint.sh scripts and airflow db upgrade commands

- Monitor containers with tools like Portainer, Prometheus, and Grafana

- Use external persistent volumes for DAGs and logs to ensure data integrity

- Log each component (webserver, scheduler, worker) separately

- Validate DAGs locally with docker-compose run --rm airflow dags list before pushing to production

Strategic Summary

Using Docker to deploy Apache Airflow in production provides a solid foundation for modern, standardized, and scalable data orchestration. With well-defined images, centralized configuration, and isolated environments, Airflow gains predictability, reproducibility, and easier maintenance. Integration with Docker Compose enables robust local environments and smooth transition to distributed environments with Celery or Kubernetes. Mastering this setup provides full control over the Airflow lifecycle, from development to large-scale operations, establishing the platform as a reliable core of corporate data engineering.

CHAPTER 14. AIRFLOW WITH KUBERNETES EXECUTOR

Apache Airflow, as a workflow orchestration platform designed for modularity, supports multiple execution strategies. Among them, the Kubernetes Executor is one of the most powerful and scalable, ideal for cloud-native environments and pipelines that require full resource isolation, operational elasticity, and execution resilience. It leverages Kubernetes resources to create an isolated pod for each task, with fine-grained control over CPU, memory allocation, environment, and mounted volumes.

When comparing the Kubernetes Executor with other execution methods, like the Celery Executor, it's clear that its adoption solves various operational limitations, at the cost of a slightly more complex initial setup. This chapter details how to configure Apache Airflow with the Kubernetes Executor, explaining the essential concepts, YAML file structure, pod template creation, task monitoring, and the main technical challenges involved in deployment on Kubernetes clusters.

Kubernetes Executor vs. Celery Executor

The Celery Executor is widely used for its flexibility, ability to distribute tasks across multiple workers, and integration with queues like Redis or RabbitMQ. However, it requires a parallel infrastructure of components—such as dedicated workers, a message broker, and a backend database—along with fine-tuned concurrency and parallelism management.

The Kubernetes Executor, on the other hand, eliminates the need for dedicated workers. Each task runs in an isolated pod, provisioned on demand by the Airflow scheduler. This model offers:

- Automatic horizontal scalability

- Total isolation between tasks

- Resource allocation per task

- Greater security through containerized isolation

- Simplified infrastructure with no need for Celery, Redis, or RabbitMQ

Feature comparison table:

- Fixed workers — Celery yes, Kubernetes no

- Required broker — Celery yes, Kubernetes no

- Execution in isolated pods — Celery no, Kubernetes yes

- Infrastructure overhead — Celery high, Kubernetes low (in cloud)

- Native elasticity — Kubernetes yes, Celery no

- Task startup time — Celery faster, Kubernetes slightly slower (due to pod creation time)

The Kubernetes Executor is ideal for modern microservices architectures, variable load environments, and organizations already running Kubernetes-managed infrastructure.

YAML Configuration and Pod Templates

Enabling the Kubernetes Executor requires specific

configurations in airflow.cfg or via environment variables, as well as proper setup of the Kubernetes environment where Airflow will run.

In airflow.cfg:

ini

```
[core]
executor = KubernetesExecutor


[kubernetes]
namespace = airflow
delete_worker_pods = True
worker_container_repository = apache/airflow
worker_container_tag = 2.7.2-python3.9
dags_in_image = False
```

For Kubernetes deployment, it's highly recommended to use the official Airflow Helm Chart, as it already provides configurable YAML templates for all components (webserver, scheduler, triggerer, etc.). Helm allows customization through values in values.yaml, where you define the executor, image, resources, and credentials.

Minimal example from values.yaml:

yaml

```
executor: KubernetesExecutor


config:
  AIRFLOW__CORE__FERNET_KEY: your_fernet_key
```

AIRFLOW__CORE__DAGS_ARE_PAUSED_AT_CREATION: 'False'

```yaml
webserver:
  service:
    type: LoadBalancer
  resources:
    limits:
      cpu: 500m
      memory: 1Gi
    requests:
      cpu: 200m
      memory: 512Mi
```

With Kubernetes Executor, Airflow creates a temporary pod for each task. The behavior of this pod is controlled by a Pod Template, which defines base image, environment variables, resource limits, volumes, sidecars, and other characteristics.

Example Pod Template YAML:

yaml

```yaml
apiVersion: v1
kind: Pod
metadata:
  name: airflow-task-template
spec:
  containers:
    - name: base
```

```yaml
    image: apache/airflow:2.7.2-python3.9
    resources:
      requests:
        memory: "512Mi"
        cpu: "500m"
      limits:
        memory: "1Gi"
        cpu: "1"
    env:
      - name: AIRFLOW__CORE__EXECUTOR
        value: KubernetesExecutor
    volumeMounts:
      - name: airflow-dags
        mountPath: /opt/airflow/dags
  volumes:
    - name: airflow-dags
      persistentVolumeClaim:
        claimName: dags-pvc
```

This template can be referenced in values.yaml to be applied to all pods automatically created by the Kubernetes Executor:

yaml

```yaml
kubernetesExecutor:
  podTemplate:
    enabled: true
```

template: airflow-task-template.yaml

Monitoring Pods and Isolated Tasks

One of the most evident advantages of the Kubernetes Executor is the detailed visibility of each task execution as a pod in the cluster. This allows real-time tracking of task status, resource consumption, logs, and failures.

Each pod created by a task is automatically named with a prefix identifying the DAG, task name, and execution date. You can list these pods with:

bash

```
kubectl get pods -n airflow
```

To view the logs of a specific task:

bash

```
kubectl logs airflow-task-sample-dag-run-abc123 -n airflow
```

Additionally, pods can be visualized in dashboards like Lens, K9s, or directly in the GKE, EKS, or AKS web interfaces. You can also set up alerts in tools like Prometheus and Grafana to monitor failures, restarts, and real-time CPU/memory usage.

The Airflow web interface still shows the DAG with its tasks, statuses, and logs, but now the logs are integrated with the cluster. They can be stored locally on the pod (with loss upon deletion), in PVCs (persistent volumes), or in storage buckets (S3, GCS), by configuring the corresponding fields in the Helm Chart.

Advantages and Challenges

Using the Kubernetes Executor offers several operational advantages:

- Elimination of the need to maintain active workers

- High scalability with pod autoscaling

- Per-task container isolation

- CPU and memory limits configuration per task

- Centralized deployment and control via Helm

- Easy integration with native Kubernetes services (ConfigMap, Secrets, PVCs)

- Better resource utilization in shared clusters

However, it also brings technical challenges:

- Longer task startup time due to pod creation

- Need for intermediate Kubernetes knowledge

- Permission and service account management for access to volumes, secrets, APIs

- Logs may be discarded if not exported to persistent destinations

- Complex initial configuration, especially regarding security and networking

- Dependency on shared storage for DAGs if they are not embedded in the image

Additionally, short-duration tasks (<5s) may be penalized by pod creation overhead. In such cases, consolidating tasks or using other executors may be more effective.

Common Error Resolution

Task pod fails to create
Check if the image is available, if resource configuration is compatible with the cluster, and if there's no permission conflict with volumes or service accounts.

Logs are not shown in the web interface
Configure the log backend to point to PVC or a persistent bucket. Set remote_logging=True and define the logging_config_class.

Permission error when mounting volume
Ensure that the service account used has access to the PVC. Create RoleBindings if necessary.

Task does not start or remains pending
The pod may be waiting for cluster resources (CPU/RAM). Run kubectl describe pod to check events and blockers.

Scheduler restarts without executing tasks
It may be a configuration conflict in Helm or an initialization error. Check the scheduler pod logs and revalidate the airflow.cfg.

Best Practices

- Create reusable Pod Templates with well-defined security and resource patterns

- Use Helm Charts with versioning to control changes and rollbacks

- Configure remote logging with GCS, S3, or Elasticsearch for log retention

- Set delete_worker_pods=True to automatically free

resources after execution

- Monitor pods with Prometheus and set automatic failure alerts

- Avoid mounting unnecessary sensitive volumes in DAGs

- Package DAGs into the image when possible to avoid PVC dependency

- Define minimum CPU and memory limits on all tasks to avoid overcommit

- Isolate staging and production environments with separate namespaces and service accounts

Strategic Summary

Adopting the Kubernetes Executor in Apache Airflow is a strategic step toward a modern, scalable, cloud-native data orchestration architecture. Creating isolated pods per task ensures maximum flexibility and control over execution resources, while simplifying infrastructure by eliminating the need for fixed workers and external message queues. Despite the initial learning curve and the challenge of correctly configuring the Kubernetes environment, the benefits in terms of elasticity, security, and observability amply justify the effort.

CHAPTER 15. ORCHESTRATING PIPELINES WITH SPARK AND HADOOP

Orchestrating pipelines in Big Data environments requires robust, scalable tools capable of interacting with different processing engines and distributed file systems. Apache Airflow, Apache Spark, and Apache Hadoop form a highly efficient ecosystem for automating complex data flows, especially those involving large volumes, multi-step transformations, and integration across distributed clusters.

Airflow connects to Spark through the SparkSubmitOperator, allowing you to trigger jobs written in Scala, Java, or PySpark directly from a DAG. Additionally, it can interact with HDFS (Hadoop Distributed File System) and other Hadoop ecosystem tools such as Hive, Pig, and HBase. Combining Airflow with Spark and Hadoop enables the construction of scalable, auditable ETL pipelines with granular control over each process stage.

This chapter presents the integration of Airflow with Spark and Hadoop, highlighting common practices in large-scale data environments, with a focus on configuration, execution, logging, diagnostics, and best practices for high-performance distributed pipelines.

Integration of Airflow with SparkSubmitOperator

The SparkSubmitOperator allows you to run Spark applications directly from Airflow DAGs, using the internal spark-submit command. It is ideal for launching jobs on running Spark clusters, whether in standalone mode, YARN, Kubernetes, or Mesos.

Basic usage example:

python

```
from airflow.providers.apache.spark.operators.spark_submit
import SparkSubmitOperator


run_spark = SparkSubmitOperator(
    task_id='run_spark_job',
    application='/opt/spark-jobs/etl_job.py',
    conn_id='spark_default',
    conf={'spark.executor.memory': '2g'},
    application_args=['--data', '/data/input/', '--output', '/data/output/'],
    dag=dag
)
```

Key parameters:

- application: path to the .py, .jar, or .scala file to run

- conn_id: Spark connection defined in Airflow

- conf: dictionary with Spark parameters (e.g., memory, parallelism, deploy mode)

- application_args: list of arguments passed to the Spark script

- executor_cores, executor_memory, driver_memory: resource configurations

The spark_default connection must be registered in Airflow with the cluster's credentials and configuration. For environments using YARN or Kubernetes, execution parameters should also reflect the deploy type (--master yarn, --master k8s://).

You can orchestrate jobs across different clusters or resource types by creating multiple connections and switching between them in DAG tasks.

Connection with HDFS and Big Data Tools

Airflow integrates with HDFS via HDFSHook and specific operators like HdfsSensor, HdfsFileSensor, HdfsToLocalOperator, and others. This allows you to monitor files, copy data, and conditionally trigger jobs.

Example of a sensor waiting for a file in HDFS:

python

```
from airflow.providers.apache.hdfs.sensors.hdfs import
HdfsSensor


wait_for_hdfs_file = HdfsSensor(
    task_id='wait_for_parquet_file',
    filepath='/raw_data/2024/file.parquet',
    hdfs_conn_id='hdfs_default',
    timeout=600,
    poke_interval=30,
    dag=dag
)
```

Beyond HDFS, Airflow can interact with Hive, Presto, HBase, and other Hadoop tools via specific hooks and operators. Example with Hive:

python

```
from airflow.providers.apache.hive.operators.hive import
HiveOperator

run_hql = HiveOperator(
    task_id='run_hive_query',
    hql='SELECT COUNT(*) FROM daily_sales;',
    hive_cli_conn_id='hive_default',
    dag=dag
)
```

This integration enables hybrid pipelines, with Spark transformations, HDFS monitoring, and Hive aggregations, all orchestrated by Airflow with declared dependencies and full tracking.

Real Use Cases for Scalable ETL

The Airflow + Spark + Hadoop combination is used in various corporate scenarios, especially:

- Batch ingestion pipelines: reading large volumes of raw data from HDFS or S3, transforming with Spark, and writing to data warehouses

- Building data lakes: orchestrating data movement and processing across bronze, silver, and gold layers with Spark jobs

- Distributed reporting: running daily or hourly Spark jobs to consolidate large-scale KPIs

- Sensor/IoT data cleaning and validation: massive processing of heterogeneous streaming data with PySpark

- Integration with external systems: orchestrating Spark jobs that perform scraping, API calls, transformations, and write to Hadoop

These pipelines typically run in environments with hundreds of parallel tasks, requiring high availability, distributed logging, and automatic reprocessing capabilities. Airflow excels by providing centralized control over these operations with full visibility and DAG reusability.

Logs and Tracking Spark Jobs

The SparkSubmitOperator integrates Spark execution logs into the Airflow interface. By clicking on an executed task, you can view the spark-submit output, including:

- Initialization time

- Driver logs

- Error or warning messages

- Prints and messages generated in PySpark code

- Application return code

In YARN or Kubernetes clusters, detailed Spark logs may be distributed across containers. In these cases, it's best to configure Spark to export logs to S3, GCS, or systems like ELK or Datadog for easier failure tracking.

Additionally, Airflow records all execution metadata:

- DAG execution_date

- Parameters passed to the Spark job

- Final status (success, failed, skipped)

- Task execution time

These details are crucial for auditing, troubleshooting, and SLA calculations.

Common Error Resolution

Spark job won't start
Check if spark-submit is correctly configured in the Airflow Docker image's path or if the cluster is accessible.

Authentication error when connecting to HDFS
Ensure the hdfs_default connection has valid credentials and that Airflow runs with proper Hadoop cluster permissions.

Spark script fails with import error
Ensure all dependencies are included in the image or in the --py-files argument of spark-submit.

Permission error writing to HDFS directory
Validate the destination directory's ACLs and permissions. You may need to configure a proxy user.

Spark logs do not appear in Airflow
In distributed environments like YARN, logs may be on the ResourceManager. Configure Spark's log backend for external redirection.

Job runs but expected output is not saved
Include post-job validation steps in the DAG, such as FileSensor,

XCom, or HDFS checks, to ensure the output was truly generated.

Best Practices

- Use SparkSubmitOperator with dynamic variables and parameters defined by Variable.get()

- Create Spark job templates with configurable arguments for reuse

- Isolate transformations by data type and aggregation type into separate DAGs

- Version Spark scripts and DAGs in separate repositories with release control

- Run automatic post-job validations with sensors or check operators

- Use pools to control load on shared Spark clusters

- Monitor Spark jobs externally with Prometheus and Grafana

- Store logs in persistent systems for later analysis

- Avoid hardcoding HDFS paths and Hive table names

- Establish naming standards for jobs, directories, DAGs, and logs

Strategic Summary

Integrating Apache Airflow with Big Data platforms like Spark and Hadoop transforms data orchestration into an intelligent, traceable, and highly scalable operation. Using the SparkSubmitOperator, connecting with HDFS, and interoperating with Hadoop ecosystem tools enables complete automation of large-scale ETL pipelines, from data ingestion to final delivery in analytical layers. With full control over dependencies, logs, resources, and reprocessing, Airflow becomes the core of corporate data governance and technical execution. By applying best practices, structuring reusable DAGs, and continuously monitoring operations, engineering teams ensure stability, performance, and continuous evolution in building data-driven solutions.

CHAPTER 16. INTEGRATIONS WITH APIS AND WEBHOOKS

Integration with APIs and Webhooks is one of the most widely used features in Apache Airflow DAGs. Through simple HTTP calls, it's possible to connect pipelines to external systems, SaaS platforms, internal microservices, and various types of RESTful endpoints. This ability to communicate via the HTTP protocol turns Airflow into a true universal automation orchestrator, enabling the execution of commands, data retrieval, and event triggering for any system with an exposed web interface.

This chapter covers integration strategies with APIs and Webhooks using the SimpleHttpOperator, sending and receiving data via HTTP methods (GET, POST, PUT, DELETE), handling payloads and headers, and key considerations when integrating with external platforms. The content focuses on practical applications, technical details, and operational best practices to ensure the robustness, security, and traceability of integrations performed by Airflow.

Using the SimpleHttpOperator

The standard operator for HTTP calls in Airflow is the SimpleHttpOperator, available in the apache-airflow-providers-http package. It enables HTTP requests to any specified endpoint, supporting common methods and the configuration of headers, parameters, payloads, and authentication.

Basic usage example:

python

```python
from airflow.providers.http.operators.http import
SimpleHttpOperator


trigger_webhook = SimpleHttpOperator(
    task_id='send_notification',
    http_conn_id='webhook_default',
    endpoint='notify/trigger',
    method='POST',
    headers={"Content-Type": "application/json"},
    data='{"event":"completed"}',
    response_check=lambda response: response.status_code ==
200,
    dag=dag
)
```

Main parameters:

- http_conn_id: identifier of the HTTP connection registered in Airflow

- endpoint: resource path within the defined host

- method: request type (GET, POST, PUT, DELETE)

- headers: dictionary with request headers

- data: request body (used in POST and PUT)

- response_check: function to validate the response

The webhook_default connection should contain the API's base host and, if necessary, basic auth or token, set in the Airflow Admin > Connections menu.

Sending Data to External Endpoints

Sending data to external APIs is a common task in pipelines that need to log events, send metrics, integrate with notification systems, or trigger automations. The SimpleHttpOperator accepts payloads in JSON, XML, or plain text formats, depending on the destination.

Example of sending job completion data:

python

```
send_result = SimpleHttpOperator(
    task_id='send_result',
    http_conn_id='api_results',
    endpoint='/api/v1/results',
    method='POST',
    headers={'Content-Type': 'application/json', 'Authorization':
'Bearer {{ var.value.api_token }}'},
    data='{"job_id": "{{ ds }}", "status": "success"}',
    dag=dag
)
```

In this case, the payload is manually built with Jinja placeholders ({{ ds }}), allowing dynamic values based on the DAG execution context.

Ensure that sent data is correctly serialized. For JSON, use json.dumps() when passing dictionaries to the data= parameter.

For sending files (such as reports or evidence), it's better to use a PythonOperator with the requests library, handling binary files with open() and multipart/form-data.

Consuming REST APIs

In addition to sending data, Airflow can consume external APIs such as weather services, market prices, catalogs, configurations, and other operational information. In this scenario, the most common method is GET, and the result can be stored in XCom for use in subsequent tasks.

Example of a GET request:

python

```python
check_price = SimpleHttpOperator(
    task_id='check_current_price',
    http_conn_id='api_prices',
    endpoint='/quote/current',
    method='GET',
    response_filter=lambda response: response.json().get("value"),
    log_response=True,
    dag=dag
)
```

The response_filter parameter allows you to directly extract part of the request result. To store the value in XCom, you can access the task return in subsequent tasks:

python

```python
price = task_instance.xcom_pull(task_ids='check_current_price')
```

GET requests with parameters are also possible via a direct URL (endpoint='quote/current?currency=USD') or by passing arguments in data (automatically converted to a query string in GET methods).

Integration with External Systems via HTTP

Many corporate platforms allow HTTP integrations: ERPs, CRMs, notification tools, monitoring systems, and more. Airflow can act as a client to these systems or receive commands through Webhooks (complemented by external tools that trigger DAGs via API).

Common HTTP integration examples:

- Trigger an Airflow DAG via POST to /api/v1/dags/ <dag_id>/dagRuns

- Notify Microsoft Teams or Slack with an error alert

- Trigger a flow in Power Automate or Integromat

- Update records in a RESTful production control API

- Publish data to REST endpoints feeding real-time dashboards

For more complex actions involving multi-step authentication (OAuth2, JWT, etc.), it's recommended to use a PythonOperator with libraries like requests, handling headers, tokens, and session renewal manually.

Common Error Resolution

Error 401 (Unauthorized)
Check if the token or authentication method is correctly defined in the connection. Dynamic tokens should be read with Variable.get() or assembled at runtime.

Request fails with status code 500
It may be an external service error. Check the validity of the parameters and body format sent.

HTTP call timeout
Increase the default value with timeout=60 in the operator or review connectivity with the remote host.

Error processing response
Ensure the response_filter or response_check properly handles the returned data types. Use try/except to capture unexpected failures.

JSON serialization failure
Always use json.dumps() when building data with dictionaries. Headers must include Content-Type: application/json.

Best Practices

- Separate connections by environment (e.g., api_prod, api_staging) and avoid manually overwriting URLs in DAGs

- Use Variable.get() for authentication tokens, avoiding hardcoding

- Validate responses with response_check to ensure successful calls

- Use parameterized DAGs for dynamic calls based on execution context

- Centralize API integration in utility modules with exception handling

- Enable `log_response=True` only in testing or non-sensitive calls

- Create dedicated pools to limit the number of simultaneous API calls on rate-limited services

- Automate token renewal with periodic operators and securely store tokens with `Variable.set()`

- Avoid exposing keys and tokens in logs or the Airflow interface

Strategic Summary

The ability to integrate with APIs and Webhooks positions Apache Airflow as a highly versatile automation tool, capable of orchestrating flows beyond just data processing. By using operators like `SimpleHttpOperator` and well-defined strategies for consuming and sending HTTP information, it becomes possible to connect Airflow to any modern external system, whether for triggering, receiving, collecting, processing, or notifying.

CHAPTER 17. LOCAL TESTING AND DAG DEBUGGING

Ensuring that DAGs are correct, functional, and error-free before deploying them to production is an essential step in data orchestration engineering with Apache Airflow. Unlike traditional systems where failures can often be easily handled through rollbacks or quick reprocessing, failures in DAG-orchestrated workflows can cause cascading impacts, corrupt data, interrupt critical flows, and undermine trust in the platform.

For this reason, every pipeline developed with Airflow must go through a phase of local testing and debugging before being promoted to the production environment. This step helps detect logic errors, parameter inconsistencies, dependency failures, and verify that the overall DAG structure behaves as expected in different execution scenarios.

This chapter covers strategies and commands for running local tests on individual tasks, validating executions with simulated data, debugging with prints, breakpoints, and log analysis. The focus is entirely on practical accuracy, emphasizing technical robustness and operational deployment safety.

airflow tasks test Command

Airflow provides the airflow tasks test command to run isolated tasks of a DAG without triggering the scheduler or altering metadata records in the database. This makes it ideal for local testing and quick checks during development.

Basic format:

bash

airflow tasks test <dag_id> <task_id> <execution_date>

Example:

bash

airflow tasks test daily_processing extract_data 2024-06-01

This command runs the extract_data task of the daily_processing DAG as if on June 1, 2024, without affecting other tasks. The execution_date can be any ISO-formatted date and will be used internally for Jinja variable interpolation.

The generated output includes:

- Complete execution logs

- Error messages (if any)

- Return values (stored in XCom)

- Available context variables

- Total execution time

This test allows you to simulate multiple scenarios by changing the execution_date, check conditional logic based on dates, and confirm whether scripts or operators are working as expected.

Debugging with Prints and Manual Logs

During DAG development, one of the simplest and most effective ways to identify unexpected behaviors is to insert output commands directly into the code. While using print() is possible, it's recommended to use Python's logging module, which offers greater control and integration with Airflow's logging system.

Example:

python

```
import logging

def transform_data(**kwargs):
    logging.info("Starting transformation")
    data = get_data()
    logging.debug(f"Raw data: {data}")
    result = process(data)
    logging.info(f"Final result: {result}")
    return result
```

Available log levels:

- logging.debug: **detailed technical use**

- logging.info: **status and progress messages**

- logging.warning: **potential issues or inconsistencies**

- logging.error: **critical execution failures**

- logging.exception: **prints error with traceback**

These logs are automatically included in task records and can be viewed both in the terminal (airflow tasks test) and the web interface after real execution.

Avoid excessive logging of sensitive data or large text volumes. For tasks handling personal data, it's best to mask or anonymize values before logging.

Using Breakpoints in VS Code

The Visual Studio Code debugger allows you to pause DAG execution at any code line and inspect variables in real time, which is extremely useful for advanced debugging. This process can be applied when the DAG or operator is being developed and run locally with airflow tasks test.

Basic steps to use breakpoints:

- Open the Python DAG code in VS Code

- Set a breakpoint by clicking to the left of the desired line

- Create a debug configuration in .vscode/launch.json:

json

```json
{
  "version": "0.2.0",
  "configurations": [
    {
      "name": "Airflow Task Debug",
      "type": "python",
      "request": "launch",
      "program": "${workspaceFolder}/venv/bin/airflow",
      "args": ["tasks", "test", "my_dag", "my_task", "2024-06-01"],
      "console": "integratedTerminal"
    }
```

```
    ]
}
```

- Start execution with F5

From there, the code will stop at the breakpoint, and you can:

- Inspect variables

- Evaluate expressions

- View the call stack

- Modify values in real time

- Step through the code with step over, step into, continue

This approach is especially useful for debugging complex operators such as API integrations, batch transformations, Spark scripts, or conditional logic in BranchPythonOperator.

Simulating Specific Executions

Beyond airflow tasks test, you can simulate complete DAG executions with airflow dags test. This command runs the entire DAG locally, without interacting with the scheduler, allowing you to test task chains and dependencies.

bash

```
airflow dags test my_dag 2024-06-01
```

This mode simulates the actual behavior of a scheduled execution in Airflow, triggering all tasks in sequence according to their dependencies. It's useful for validating whether the

DAG:

- Is structured correctly

- Has well-defined dependencies

- Has no loops or chaining errors

- Behaves as expected under different dates

If you want to test only part of the DAG (for example, a branch), you can use Trigger Rules and DAG params to force specific paths.

You can also use the dag_run.conf feature in controlled tests to pass custom parameters to the DAG at runtime.

Common Error Resolution

ImportError when running task
Check if all dependencies are installed in the active virtual environment. Use pip freeze to confirm.

Malformed DAG error
Ensure the dag_id is correct and there are no indentation or syntax errors. Run airflow dags list to list recognized DAGs.

None value in XCom
The task function may not be returning anything or the returned value may not be serializable. Confirm with an explicit return.

Jinja variable error
Jinja only works with execution_date or ds if the DAG is in execution context. Use airflow tasks test with a valid date.

Breakpoints not working
Check if VS Code is pointing to the correct virtual environment and if the task is being started inside the debugger.

Task not showing in the graph
There may be an error in task chaining. Review the use of `>>`, `set_upstream()`, or conditional dependencies.

Best Practices

- Use airflow tasks test whenever task logic changes

- Configure structured logging with logging.info() for easier analysis

- Test multiple execution_date values to simulate different contexts

- Write modular DAG scripts with externally testable functions

- Keep variables and connections outside the code, accessing them via Variable.get() and BaseHook.get_connection()

- Document what each task expects and returns to aid log reading

- Control exceptions with try/except and log clear messages

- Validate returned data types to ensure XCom compatibility

- Use descriptive task and DAG names for easier tracking

- Automate tests with tools like pytest or CI/CD commands using airflow tasks test

Strategic Summary

The local testing and debugging phase for Airflow DAGs is essential to ensure the stability and predictability of pipelines before they go live. By mastering tools like airflow tasks test, airflow dags test, manual logs, and breakpoints, developers gain full control over the behavior of their DAGs in any execution scenario.

This approach drastically reduces production failures, avoids rework, and increases stakeholder confidence in the created automations.

CHAPTER 18. JINJA TEMPLATES AND MACROS

The use of Jinja templates and macros in Apache Airflow represents one of the most powerful features for making DAGs and tasks highly dynamic, parameterized, and adaptable to different execution contexts. These resources allow strings, commands, scripts, and even operator arguments to be interpreted based on the context of each DAG run, using variables such as execution date, run IDs, formatted timestamps, execution intervals, and other elements automatically provided by the Airflow scheduler.

With Jinja and macros, you can avoid hardcoding, build file paths based on dates, parameterize SQL queries, generate unique file names, automate executions based on time windows, among many other possibilities. This results in cleaner, more reusable, and robust DAGs.

This chapter explores the practical application of Jinja templates, the complete set of available macros, the use of contextual variables provided by Airflow, strategies for automating dynamic parameters, and real-world application examples, focusing entirely on technical precision, operational clarity, and orchestration engineering best practices.

Applying Jinja in Parameters

Airflow uses the Jinja2 templating engine to interpret operator fields marked as "templated." These fields accept expressions wrapped in {{ ... }} that will be evaluated at the time of the DAG execution, based on the task context.

Basic example with BashOperator:

python

```
from airflow.operators.bash import BashOperator

task = BashOperator(
    task_id='list_files',
    bash_command='ls /data/input/{{ ds }}',
    dag=dag
)
```

In this example, the value of {{ ds }} (execution date in YYYY-MM-DD format) will be dynamically replaced at each DAG run. If the DAG runs on 2024-06-01, the resulting command will be:

bash

```
ls /data/input/2024-06-01
```

This feature allows you to build paths, file names, SQL commands, and URLs based on the current DAG execution without additional Python logic.

Fields that support templates include:

- bash_command in **BashOperator**

- sql in **PostgresOperator, BigQueryOperator, HiveOperator, and others**

- data in **SimpleHttpOperator**

- file_path in **PythonVirtualenvOperator, PythonOperator**

- params in any operator

Available Macros and Contextual Variables

Airflow provides a set of macros — utility functions — that can be used inside templates to manipulate dates, executions, DAG metadata, and other useful functions.

Main available macros:

- {{ ds }}: execution date (e.g., 2024-06-01)

- {{ ds_nodash }}: date without dashes (e.g., 20240601)

- {{ ts }}: execution timestamp (e.g., 2024-06-01T00:00:00+00:00)

- {{ ts_nodash }}: timestamp without dashes

- {{ prev_ds }}: previous execution date

- {{ next_ds }}: next execution date

- {{ dag }}: current DAG object

- {{ task }}: current Task object

- {{ run_id }}: unique identifier of the DAG Run

- {{ execution_date }}: execution datetime object (more complete than ds)

- {{ macros.ds_add(ds, n) }}: date resulting from adding/subtracting n days

- {{ macros.datetime.utcnow() }}: **current UTC timestamp**

- {{ macros.json.dumps(obj) }}: **serializes JSON object**

These macros are automatically available in the scope of each task when rendering the template. You can also define custom macros and add them to the execution context through advanced configurations.

Automating Dynamic Parameters

One of the major advantages of using Jinja templates is the ability to generate dynamic parameters that automatically adapt to the execution date without requiring additional coding.

Example with PythonOperator and params:

python

```python
def load_file(**kwargs):
    path = kwargs['params']['path']
    print(f"Reading file from: {path}")


dynamic_task = PythonOperator(
    task_id='read_file',
    python_callable=load_file,
    params={'path': '/data/input/{{ ds }}/file.csv'},
    dag=dag
)
```

In this example, the params['path'] field will automatically resolve to /data/input/2024-06-01/file.csv when the DAG runs on the corresponding date. This approach is useful for abstracting logic and reusing operators without rewriting code.

Another example with dynamic SQL:

python

```
query = PostgresOperator(
    task_id='query_data',
    postgres_conn_id='postgres_default',
    sql='SELECT * FROM sales WHERE sale_date = DATE \'{{ ds }}
\'",
    dag=dag
)
```

This type of parameterization is ideal for versioned SQL scripts or scripts reused by multiple DAGs.

Practical Cases with Date-Based Execution

Macros and templates are extremely useful for cases where the pipeline needs to act based on the execution date:

- File paths: reading and writing in date-partitioned directories

- SQL queries: time-based filters using execution date

- Exported file names: adding timestamps to filenames

- Organizing logs and reports: saving outputs with unique names

- API triggers: passing dynamic parameters like start_date and end_date

Example of filename with timestamp:

python

```
export = BashOperator(
    task_id='export_csv',
    bash_command='python export.py --output /results/
report_{{ ts_nodash }}.csv',
    dag=dag
)
```

The resulting file will be named like report_20240601T000000.csv, unique per execution.

Another example with S3 partitioning:

python

```
upload = PythonOperator(
    task_id='send_to_s3',
    python_callable=send_to_s3,
    op_kwargs={'destination_folder': 's3://bucket/datalake/
{{ ds }}/'},
    dag=dag
)
```

This type of logic makes the pipeline fully time-adaptive without the need for if statements or manual string formatting.

Common Error Resolution

Jinja field not interpreted

Ensure the field is quoted and that the operator supports templating on that field. Not all attributes are automatically rendered.

UndefinedError: 'ds' is undefined
The template is being evaluated outside the execution context. Only use inside operators with actual execution or use airflow tasks test.

Incorrectly rendered parameter
Check that the macro is wrapped in {{ }} and that there are no unwanted spaces or line breaks. Macros are formatting-sensitive.

Wrong execution data in scripts
Ensure the variable used matches the expected format. ds is a string, execution_date is a datetime object. Use .strftime() if needed.

Failure when running DAG with Jinja in parameters
Fields unsupported by templates (like task_id, dag_id) should not contain {{ }}. Use direct variables for these fields.

Best Practices

- Always check if the field supports template_fields before using Jinja

- Use standard macros like ds, ts, run_id to identify executions

- Avoid hardcoding paths, filenames, and filter parameters

- Document template usage in comments within the code

- Validate rendering with airflow tasks render before

running the DAG

- Modularize external commands to accept dynamic arguments

- Store custom macros in separate utilities and import them as needed

- Avoid complex formatting logic directly in templates—use Python functions whenever possible

Strategic Summary

Jinja templates and macros in Apache Airflow offer an advanced flexibility layer for building intelligent, parameterized, and adaptable DAGs for various execution contexts. They allow transforming static pipelines into dynamic flows driven by time, rules, and contextual variables without needing to modify the source code for each new execution.

By mastering the use of {{ ds }}, {{ ts }}, {{ macros.ds_add }}, and other template tools, data engineers can structure more reusable, error-resistant, and maintainable DAGs that scale efficiently. With best practices, validation, and organized code, templates become a solid bridge between the orchestration of technical processes and the adaptation of workflows to real business needs.

CHAPTER 19. SECURITY IN AIRFLOW

Security is one of the fundamental pillars in orchestrating data workflows in corporate environments. In Apache Airflow, the need to control who can view, modify, or execute DAGs, as well as protect sensitive credentials and variables, is critical to operational integrity, data confidentiality, and compliance with security policies such as LGPD, GDPR, HIPAA, among others.

This chapter provides a detailed guide on implementing robust security in Airflow, covering key mechanisms of authentication and authorization, user and role management with RBAC, protection of sensitive data such as connections and variables, and secure engineering best practices for production environments. The goal is to equip the reader to configure a secure, auditable, and resilient Airflow environment against unauthorized access or exposure failures.

Authentication and Authorization

The authentication layer defines how users identify themselves in the system. Airflow supports several authentication mechanisms such as:

- Default username/password authentication (local database)

- LDAP/Active Directory authentication

- Google OAuth, GitHub, Auth0, Okta authentication

- JWT (JSON Web Token) authentication

- Enterprise SSO (Single Sign-On)

Configuration is done in the webserver_config.py file, where the authentication backend is defined using the AUTH_BACKEND variable.

Example with password authentication (default):

python

```
from airflow.www.security import AirflowSecurityManager
AUTH_BACKEND = 'airflow.www.security.DefaultAuthBackend'
```

Example with OAuth using Google:

python

```
AUTH_BACKEND =
'airflow.www.security.oauth2_auth.OAuth2PasswordBearer'
```

OAuth support requires additional configuration in webserver_config.py, including client_id, client_secret, and authorized scopes.

In addition to authentication, Airflow includes a role-based authorization system (RBAC - Role-Based Access Control) that allows precise control over which resources each user or group can access. This system defines:

- Actions: view, edit, create, delete, execute

- Objects: DAGs, tasks, connections, variables, users, logs

- Roles: sets of permissions assigned to users

User and Role Management

Users can be created via the web interface, CLI, or Python scripts using Airflow's internal API.

Via interface:

- Go to Admin > Users

- Click + to add a new user

- Fill in name, email, username, password, and assign a role

Via CLI:

bash

```
airflow users create \
  --username operator \
  --firstname John \
  --lastname Doe \
  --role User \
  --email john@company.com
```

Default Airflow roles include:

- Admin: full system access

- User: access to DAGs, no connection or global config management

- Op (Operator): can run DAGs, view logs, no code editing

- Viewer: read-only access to DAGs and logs

- Public: minimal access, usually disabled in private environments

Custom roles can also be created by grouping specific permissions. This is done in the interface under Admin > Roles, where profiles can be built based on real needs, such as:

- DataAnalyst: can run read-only DAGs and view task logs

- DataEngineer: can edit DAGs, create connections and variables

- DevOps: can pause DAGs and monitor scheduler failures

Users can have multiple roles, enabling flexible privilege management without redundancy.

RBAC and Access Control

The RBAC system is enabled by default in recent Airflow versions. In older versions, activation is done in airflow.cfg:

ini

```
[webserver]
rbac = True
```

With RBAC enabled, every action performed via the interface or API is subject to a permission check. This means that a user without the "Can Edit on DAG" right cannot edit a DAG's code even if they can access the interface.

Key permission objects:

- DAGs (by ID or wildcard)

- Connections

- Variables

- Pools

- Task Instances

- XCom

- Configuration

- Plugins

Access can be granted per individual DAG, allowing different teams to operate separate DAGs without conflict or exposure risk.

Model of segmented policy:

- Finance team can access only DAGs with the prefix fin_

- Data engineering team can edit etl_ and raw_ DAGs

- Business users can only view logs and pause executions

This refined control is ideal for multi-user, multi-team environments with different operational responsibilities over pipelines.

Protecting Sensitive Variables

Airflow stores variables and connections in the metadata database. This information may include credentials, API tokens, database connection strings, and operational secrets. By default, all variables and connections are visible to any user with interface access, posing a risk.

To protect this information, Airflow offers:

- Fernet Key encryption: values are encrypted before being saved in the database

- Hidden sensitive fields: passwords and tokens are marked as hidden and do not appear in logs

- Sensitive variables: values marked as "hidden" when creating a variable

The Fernet Key must be set in airflow.cfg:

ini

```
[core]
fernet_key = your_generated_key_here
```

The key can be generated with:

bash

```
python -c "from cryptography.fernet import Fernet;
print(Fernet.generate_key().decode())"
```

Additionally, secret management can be moved to external systems like AWS Secrets Manager, HashiCorp Vault, Azure Key Vault, and Google Secret Manager using the secrets_backend parameter in airflow.cfg or in the Helm Chart values.yaml.

This approach ensures that secrets are not stored in the metadata database and that access is auditable and managed by external policies.

Common Error Resolution

User can access other teams' DAGs
Check if the RBAC policy is properly applied. Remove Admin role if not needed.

Error 403 when accessing the interface
User may lack minimum read permission. Assign a role with at least Viewer access.

Password stored shows in the variable field
When creating variables with tokens or passwords, mark them as "hidden" or migrate to an encrypted secrets backend.

Error when creating users via CLI
Ensure the metadata database is initialized and the specified role exists. Use airflow roles list to check.

Invalid OAuth token
Revalidate callback and scope configurations in the OAuth provider. Ensure endpoints are correct.

Best Practices

- Enable RBAC on all Airflow instances

- Use OAuth or LDAP authentication for corporate environments

- Create custom roles based on actual user needs

- Avoid using the Admin role as the default for new users

- Apply the principle of least privilege

- Store secrets in external solutions, not in Airflow variables

- Monitor user, DAG, and connection changes with external auditing

- Use Fernet encryption with periodically rotated keys

- Avoid logging sensitive secrets or variables in operators

- Periodically review access and assigned permissions

Strategic Summary

Security in Apache Airflow must be treated as a priority from the early stages of deployment and development. With robust authentication mechanisms, fine-grained RBAC access control, encryption of sensitive data, and integration with external identity and secret providers, Airflow can be operated with high confidence even in regulated and critical environments.

By adopting a best-practice approach with role segregation, least privilege policies, and active auditing, the platform remains resilient against unauthorized access, accidental data exposure, and operational errors.

CHAPTER 20. AIRFLOW REST API

Apache Airflow provides a powerful REST API that allows you to control and interact with almost all platform resources programmatically. The REST API, especially version 2 (API v2), is based on modern, well-defined standards, supporting operations such as creating, updating, running, and deleting DAGs, tasks, connections, and variables. This enables process automation, integration with external systems, implementation of self-adjusting pipelines, and building custom dashboards for monitoring.

The Airflow REST API allows external systems, web applications, orchestration scripts, and CI/CD tools to interact directly with the data orchestration environment without manual intervention through the interface. By mastering this communication layer, data engineers gain a new dimension of control and operational efficiency.

This chapter presents the main features of the Airflow API v2, details the supported methods, shows how to make GET, POST, and DELETE calls, and guides the construction of secure and practical external automations, along with concrete examples and best practices.

Available Endpoints in API v2

The Airflow API v2 is available in all recent versions and follows the OpenAPI (Swagger) standard, allowing navigation through a graphical interface and automatic documentation. It is available at the default path:

ruby

http://<airflow_host>:8080/api/v1/

And the Swagger documentation is accessed at:

bash

http://<airflow_host>:8080/api/v1/ui/

Main available endpoints:

- /dags: list, create, update, and delete DAGs

- /dags/{dag_id}/dagRuns: manage DAG executions

- /dags/{dag_id}/tasks: access and manage tasks in a DAG

- /dags/{dag_id}/dagRuns/{dag_run_id}/taskInstances: status of running tasks

- /variables: create, list, and delete variables

- /connections: manage connections (conn_id)

- /pools: query and change execution pools

- /config: get configuration parameters

- /users: create and list users (if enabled)

Each endpoint supports different HTTP methods (GET, POST, PATCH, DELETE) depending on its specific function.

GET, POST, and DELETE Methods

The use of HTTP methods follows the RESTful standard. The GET method is used for querying, POST for creating, PATCH for partial updates, and DELETE for removing records.

Example using curl to list all DAGs:

bash

```
curl -X GET "http://localhost:8080/api/v1/dags" -H
"Authorization: Basic base64user:password"
```

Example of creating a DAG execution (manual trigger):

bash

```
curl -X POST "http://localhost:8080/api/v1/dags/etl_daily/
dagRuns" \
  -H "Content-Type: application/json" \
  -H "Authorization: Basic base64user:password" \
  -d '{"conf": {"input_parameter": "value"}}'
```

To delete a variable:

bash

```
curl   -X   DELETE   "http://localhost:8080/api/v1/variables/
secret_token" \
  -H "Authorization: Basic base64user:password"
```

For authenticated calls, the simplest method is Basic Authentication with Authorization: Basic, but in corporate environments, it is highly recommended to use token-based authentication (Bearer) or OAuth2 integration.

External Automation via API

With the Airflow REST API, you can implement a series of external automations, such as:

- Automatic triggering of DAGs by external systems (ERP, CRM, monitoring systems)

- Periodic collection of DAG statuses for internal dashboards

- Creation of temporary or parameterized DAGs by ingestion systems

- Synchronization of variables and connections from a secure repository

- Integration with CI/CD tools for continuous deployment of DAGs

- Programmatic registration and removal of connections to databases, APIs, and analytical systems

These automations increase team autonomy, reduce manual errors, and allow Airflow to act as an operational core in broader architectures.

Example of System Integration

A common case is integration with a file ingestion system that, upon detecting the arrival of a new data batch, triggers a specific DAG in Airflow.

Python code with requests:

python

```python
import requests
import json
```

```
url = "http://localhost:8080/api/v1/dags/ingestion_batch/
dagRuns"
headers = {
    "Content-Type": "application/json",
    "Authorization": "Basic base64user:password"
}

data = {
    "conf": {
        "file": "batch_20240601.csv",
        "source": "sftp_client"
    }
}

response = requests.post(url, headers=headers,
data=json.dumps(data))

if response.status_code == 200:
    print("DAG successfully triggered.")
else:
    print(f"Error: {response.status_code} - {response.text}")
```

Another example is creating a custom web interface where business users can manually trigger a DAG without accessing Airflow. This interface sends a POST request to the /

dags/{dag_id}/dagRuns endpoint with the desired parameters, simplifying usage for non-technical profiles.

Common Error Resolution

Error 403 (Forbidden) when accessing API
The user does not have sufficient permissions. Confirm that the assigned role allows API actions. RBAC must be properly configured.

Error 401 (Unauthorized)
Invalid username or password, or expired token. In OAuth-authenticated environments, verify that the token is correct and valid.

Failure to create dagRun
Check if the dag_id exists, if the DAG is enabled, and if the parameters sent are correctly defined in the conf field.

Error 500 (Internal Server Error) when querying tasks
It may be a communication problem with the metadata database or a corrupted DAG. Check the webserver and scheduler logs.

Variable not found after creation
Creating variables via API is immediate, but some DAGs may need a refresh or scheduler restart to recognize new variables depending on the configuration.

Best Practices

- Enable only the endpoints necessary for each external application

- Use authentication tokens instead of fixed credentials

- Monitor API usage with logs and alerts to identify abuses

or failures

- Validate the data sent in the conf fields to avoid execution errors

- Define quotas or request limits per IP or application

- Document the endpoints used in each integration with practical examples

- Use tools like Postman or Swagger UI to test and validate calls before final automation

- Avoid exposing the Airflow API to the public internet — use proxies or internal VPNs

- Segment access with dedicated roles for integration (e.g., CI, Ingestion_API) with minimal permissions

- Version integration scripts and maintain separate logs of API calls

Strategic Summary

The Apache Airflow REST API v2 transforms the platform into a true automation and integration hub, enabling programmatic control of DAGs, executions, variables, connections, and tasks. With it, you can connect Airflow to any corporate system, trigger pipelines on demand, collect operational data for visualization, manage resources remotely, and enable advanced automations with full traceability.

CHAPTER 21. DAG VERSIONING

DAG versioning is an essential practice to ensure traceability, change control, operational integrity, and consistency across environments when using Apache Airflow. In data engineering projects with multiple teams and production pipelines, the code that defines the workflows must always be under strict change control. Airflow, being a Python-based platform, directly supports this approach through integration with version control systems like Git.

Adopting versioning practices for DAGs not only improves team collaboration but also reduces production failures, allows immediate rollback of changes, facilitates code reviews, and enables continuous integration and delivery (CI/CD) processes. This chapter presents in-depth Git control mechanisms, branch strategies for distinct environments, automated deployment practices, ways to monitor changes in production, and measures to ensure governance in the lifecycle of pipelines orchestrated by Airflow.

Git Control

Using Git to version DAGs is one of the most fundamental practices in managing pipelines with Airflow. All content in the dags/ directory, as well as auxiliary scripts, configuration files, and plugins, must be stored in a Git repository.

The minimal versioning structure can follow this model:

/airflow-dags

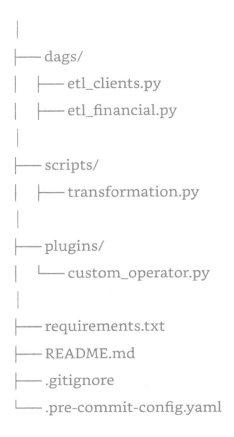

```
│
├── dags/
│   ├── etl_clients.py
│   ├── etl_financial.py
│
├── scripts/
│   ├── transformation.py
│
├── plugins/
│   └── custom_operator.py
│
├── requirements.txt
├── README.md
├── .gitignore
└── .pre-commit-config.yaml
```

Every change made to any DAG must be recorded as a descriptive commit. This allows the change history to be tracked, multiple developers to work in parallel, and the code to go through validation processes before going into production.

In addition to simple versioning, best practices include:

- Use git tag to mark DAG release versions

- Apply commit message conventions (e.g., Conventional Commits)

- Adopt pre-commits for linting, syntax checking, and template validation

- Avoid direct commits to the main branch (use merge requests/pull requests with review)

The use of Git brings security and predictability to the development cycle, transforming the DAG into a managed component like any other corporate source code.

Branch Strategies per Environment

In professional environments, there are usually multiple Airflow execution environments: development (dev), staging, and production (prod). Each of these environments can receive DAGs at different times according to the test and validation flow.

The most common strategy is to use specific branches for each environment:

- main or prod: validated code in production

- staging: code in integrated testing phase

- develop: active development branch

- feature branches: for each new DAG or specific change

Typical flow:

- The developer creates a new DAG or changes an existing one in the develop branch

- After local tests and review, merges into the staging branch

- The DAG is tested in staging with real data but without impacting the system

- After validation, the code is promoted to main or prod via merge

This model favors the stability of the production environment while allowing continuous innovation with safety. Protections can be added to branches via policies in GitHub, GitLab, or Bitbucket, requiring mandatory reviews or peer approval.

Automated Deployment with CI/CD

Once the DAGs are versioned in Git, the natural next step is to automate their deployment with continuous integration and delivery (CI/CD) tools. The typical CI/CD process for Airflow involves:

- Code validation (linting, tests, Jinja templates)

- Automatic deployment of approved DAGs to the Airflow server

- Update of the dags/ directory in the target environment

- Restart (when necessary) of the scheduler or refresh trigger

CI/CD pipeline with GitHub Actions:

yaml

```
name: Deploy DAGs to Production

on:
  push:
    branches:
      - main
```

```
jobs:
  deploy:
    runs-on: ubuntu-latest
    steps:
      - uses: actions/checkout@v2

      - name: Deploy DAGs via SSH
        uses: appleboy/scp-action@master
        with:
          host: ${{ secrets.HOST }}
          username: ${{ secrets.USERNAME }}
          key: ${{ secrets.SSH_KEY }}
          source: "dags/"
          target: "/opt/airflow/dags/"
```

In containerized environments, deployment can be done with Docker image rebuild:

bash

```
docker build -t airflow-prod:latest .
docker push registry.example.com/airflow-prod
kubectl rollout restart deployment airflow-webserver
```

This model enables automated deployment with every merge into main, with change history and fast rollback in case of failure.

Common tools for CI/CD with Airflow include:

- GitHub Actions

- GitLab CI

- Jenkins

- Bitbucket Pipelines

- ArgoCD (in Kubernetes environments)

Monitoring Changes in Production

Controlling changes in production is essential to ensure stability and traceability. Some best monitoring practices include:

- Enable audit logs to list who modified DAGs, when, and with what content

- Monitor the dags/ directory with tools like inotify, Prometheus Exporters, or custom scripts

- Create audit DAGs that list, compare, and validate the current content of DAGs on the server

- Store run_id and dag_run.conf for each execution for later tracking

- Validate if DAGs in production match the latest version from the main branch using hash comparison scripts

- Keep automatic backups of production DAGs (e.g., daily zips of the dags/ directory)

This way, it is possible to detect unauthorized manual deployments, branch divergence, and accidental changes.

Common Error Resolution

DAG does not appear after deployment
Check if the .py file is in the correct directory and without syntax errors. Use airflow dags list to confirm.

Jinja template does not render correctly
The field using the macro may not be marked as template_fields. Redefine the operator or add logs with logging.info().

Error when uploading new DAG with duplicate name
The dag_id must be unique in the cluster. Remove old DAGs or change the identifier.

CI fails on push
Confirm that the SSH key is correctly configured in the CI/CD tool's secrets and that the remote host accepts the connection.

Automatic container rollout does not update DAGs
Check if the mounted directory contains updated files or if the persistent volume is overwriting the dags folder.

Best Practices

- Store all DAG code in Git with complete history

- Keep scripts, configs, and plugins in the same repository (or submodules)

- Create CI/CD pipelines with validation before deployment

- Implement branches per environment and approval policies

- Use tags or releases to mark deployed versions

- Apply linters and automatic validators on airflow dags list, airflow tasks test, airflow dags check

- Also store versioned DAGs in production backups

- Audit DAGs with tools or internal validation DAGs

- Define naming conventions, folders, and code templates

- Standardize commit messages for easy change tracking

Strategic Summary

Versioning DAGs in Apache Airflow is not just a recommended practice, but a necessity for environments that value stability, traceability, and governance. The use of Git as the control base, combined with smart branching strategies, continuous integration, and automated deployment, establishes a modern, reliable, and scalable data engineering culture.

By ensuring that all changes to DAGs go through review, validation, and automatic tracking, teams increase the quality of pipelines, reduce production incidents, and can evolve their workflows safely. Airflow integrates perfectly with modern DevOps tools, allowing data workflows to be treated with the same technical rigor applied to professional software development.

CHAPTER 22. SCALING WITH CELERY EXECUTOR

The Celery Executor is one of the most robust and scalable options in Apache Airflow for environments requiring intensive parallelism, load distribution, and high availability. Its distributed architecture allows the execution of tasks across multiple workers, spread over different physical servers or containers, while the scheduler remains centralized. Communication between components is mediated by a message broker such as Redis or RabbitMQ, which provides resilience and decoupling between orchestration and execution processes.

Unlike the LocalExecutor — which runs all tasks on the same scheduler host — the Celery Executor distributes tasks across workers that can scale horizontally according to demand. This is essential for pipelines with multiple DAGs, intense parallel execution, and the need to isolate critical tasks.

In this chapter, we will deeply explore the Celery Executor architecture, configuration of the components involved, choosing between Redis or RabbitMQ as a broker, load balancing strategies, performance optimizations, troubleshooting, and best practices for large-scale Airflow environments.

Celery Distributed Architecture

The Celery Executor architecture in Airflow consists of the following elements:

- Scheduler: responsible for deciding which tasks should run and when. It does not execute tasks; it only sends commands to the broker.

- Message Broker (Redis or RabbitMQ): receives scheduler commands and queues the tasks for execution.

- Celery Workers: instances that listen to the broker and execute tasks when they receive them. Each worker can process multiple tasks simultaneously, according to its CPU and memory capacity.

- Result Backend (metadatabase): where task results, logs, states, and metadata are stored and queried.

Operational Flow:

- The scheduler identifies that a task is ready for execution.

- It sends a message to the broker with the task instructions.

- An available Celery worker reads the message from the broker and executes the task.

- The task state (success, failed, etc.) is reported back to the metadatabase.

- The Airflow Web UI reflects the updated status to the user.

This separation allows workers to scale horizontally as the load increases, so failures in one worker do not affect others, and the system remains functional even with thousands of tasks being processed simultaneously.

Redis or RabbitMQ as Broker

The Celery Executor requires a message broker to mediate communication between the scheduler and workers. The two officially supported brokers are Redis and RabbitMQ. The choice between them should consider the use case, the team's familiarity with the technology, and the reliability and performance requirements.

- Redis: simpler to configure, good performance for standard workloads, ideal for small to medium clusters. Can be used in standalone mode or as a cluster.

- RabbitMQ: more robust architecture, advanced support for queues, exchanges, message routing, and high availability. Better suited for critical environments with multiple queues and complex routing.

Configuration in airflow.cfg (example with Redis):

ini

```
[core]
executor = CeleryExecutor


[celery]
broker_url = redis://redis_host:6379/0
result_backend = db+postgresql://
airflow:password@postgres_host/airflow
```

Example with RabbitMQ:

ini

```
[celery]
broker_url = amqp://airflow:password@rabbitmq_host:5672/
airflow
```

Both brokers must be accessible to all components of the Airflow cluster (scheduler and all workers). It is highly recommended that the broker be on a dedicated, monitored host with strong authentication and TLS encryption enabled.

Load Balancing Among Workers

In an environment with multiple Celery workers, load balancing naturally occurs through the message queue. Each worker consumes tasks according to its availability. However, behavior can be fine-tuned using specific configurations:

- worker_concurrency: maximum number of tasks executed simultaneously per worker.

- worker_prefetch_multiplier: how many tasks the worker pulls from the broker at once (default: 4).

- task_acks_late: defines if the worker acknowledges task execution only after its completion (recommended: True).

- worker_max_tasks_per_child: maximum number of tasks before restarting the worker process (prevents memory leaks).

Model in airflow.cfg:

ini

```
[celery]
worker_concurrency = 8
worker_prefetch_multiplier = 1
task_acks_late = True
worker_max_tasks_per_child = 100
```

It is also possible to create specific queues with queue= in the operators and configure workers dedicated to processing only certain queues, promoting isolation between critical and secondary workloads.

Example:

python

```
from airflow.operators.bash import BashOperator


task = BashOperator(
    task_id='process_critical',
    bash_command='process_data.sh',
    queue='critical_queue',
    dag=dag
)
```

Worker listening only to the queue:

bash

```
airflow celery worker -q critical_queue
```

This approach allows resource segmentation and ensures that priority tasks are not stuck in queues congested by less important processes.

Performance Tuning

For environments with high execution rates, heavy DAGs, or large volumes of data processed, it is necessary to apply optimizations to the Airflow cluster:

- Enable asynchronous logging (remote_logging = True) to avoid local disk overload.

- **Adjust** parallelism, dag_concurrency, and max_active_runs_per_dag to reflect the workers' actual capacity.

- **Increase** sql_alchemy_pool_size and sql_alchemy_max_overflow in the metadata database to handle multiple simultaneous connections.

- Use Redis in cluster mode for greater fault tolerance.

- Monitor worker CPU and RAM usage with Prometheus + Grafana.

- Package heavy DAGs and operators into optimized Docker images to reduce startup time.

- **Configure** celeryd_autoscale in native Celery environments to automatically activate/deactivate workers based on demand.

DAG with optimized parallel tasks:

python

```python
with DAG('etl_multiprocess', max_active_runs=3,
concurrency=20) as dag:
    tasks = []
    for i in range(20):
        tasks.append(BashOperator(
            task_id=f'process_{i}',
            bash_command=f'echo "Processing {i}"',
            queue='default'
        ))
```

Common Error Resolution

Tasks stuck in queued state
Check if there are active workers listening to the correct queue.
Confirm if the broker is online and accepting connections.

Broker connection error
Ensure that the Redis or RabbitMQ host and port are accessible from the workers' containers/hosts. Use fixed IPs or valid DNS names.

Workers run but do not report status
There may be an error in the result_backend. Check if the database is accessible and if the workers have write permissions.

Celery worker keeps restarting
Possible memory failure, too many simultaneous tasks, or a leak in the task code. Adjust worker_concurrency and worker_max_tasks_per_child.

"Task not found" message in the log
The task was removed or the DAG was changed without updating the image/container. Restart the workers or clear the DAG cache.

Best Practices

- Use dedicated workers for specific queues (e.g., high_priority, long_duration)

- Monitor the broker with tools like redis-cli, rabbitmqctl, or Prometheus

- Configure alerts for stuck DAGs, congested queues, and inactive workers

- Automate the deployment of new workers with Docker Compose, Kubernetes, or Ansible

- Keep task_acks_late = True to avoid losing tasks after a worker failure

- Use max_active_runs_per_dag with realistic limits based on load testing

- Create observability dashboards for DAGs, queues, workers, and average execution time

- Document the execution architecture and adopted scaling policies

- Avoid complex conditional logic inside tasks — prefer explicit branching with BranchPythonOperator

- Use tags and naming conventions to track DAGs in environments with multiple clusters

Strategic Summary

The Celery Executor positions Apache Airflow as a truly scalable, resilient data orchestration platform suitable for mission-critical environments. Its distributed architecture allows tasks to be executed in parallel by multiple workers, supporting variable loads efficiently and flexibly. Using brokers like Redis or RabbitMQ ensures decoupling and reliability in component communication, while tuning strategies and queue segmentation optimize the use of available resources.

By mastering the configuration of the Celery Executor, the data engineer gains full control over pipeline execution, being able to scale horizontally according to demand, isolate critical tasks, maintain high availability, and ensure consistent delivery in dynamic environments. When well-tuned with the Celery Executor, Airflow becomes the heart of corporate intelligent data automation, ready to operate at scale with robustness and governance.

CHAPTER 23. ADVANCED LOGGING AND AUDITING

Apache Airflow, as a data orchestration platform, requires a robust logging infrastructure and reliable auditing mechanisms to ensure traceability, efficient diagnostics, and compliance with corporate and regulatory policies. In production environments, logs are the main source of evidence for investigating failures, validating executions, and proving the integrity of data flows. When combined with advanced auditing practices, logging systems also become central elements in operational governance and access control.

In this module, we will explore advanced logging capabilities in Airflow, including external log backend configuration, integration with the ELK Stack (Elasticsearch, Logstash, Kibana), execution auditing strategies, log retention and rotation techniques, as well as troubleshooting and essential best practices to keep operations auditable, traceable, and secure.

External Log Configuration

By default, Airflow stores task logs locally in the directory:

php

```
~/airflow/logs/<dag_id>/<task_id>/<execution_date>/
```

In environments with multiple workers or distributed executors (Celery, Kubernetes), this model becomes limited, as each instance maintains its own files. To solve this, Airflow allows configuring remote logging, directing logs to external backends like Amazon S3, Google Cloud Storage, Azure Blob Storage, or Elasticsearch.

Remote logging is enabled in the airflow.cfg file:

ini

```
[logging]
remote_logging = True
remote_log_conn_id = s3_logs
remote_base_log_folder = s3://airflow-logs
encrypt_s3_logs = False
logging_level = INFO
```

Or with Google Cloud:

ini

```
remote_log_conn_id = google_cloud_default
remote_base_log_folder = gs://airflow-logs
```

Additionally, ensure the referenced connection (conn_id) is correctly configured with valid credentials.

Airflow automatically uploads logs at the end of each task, ensuring centralization, persistence, and accessibility. This is essential in Kubernetes or multi-node environments where local logs can be ephemeral.

Integration with ELK Stack

The ELK Stack (Elasticsearch, Logstash, Kibana) is one of the most complete observability solutions, combining data indexing (Elastic), transformation and ingestion (Logstash), and visualization (Kibana). Integrating Airflow with ELK enables storing structured logs, performing detailed searches, and visualizing metrics in real time.

Integration steps:

- Configure Elasticsearch as the log backend

In airflow.cfg:

ini

```
remote_logging = True

logging_config_class =
custom_logging_config.LOGGING_CONFIG
```

Create a custom file custom_logging_config.py with the content:

python

```
from airflow.config_templates.airflow_local_settings import
DEFAULT_LOGGING_CONFIG

import os


LOGGING_CONFIG = DEFAULT_LOGGING_CONFIG.copy()


LOGGING_CONFIG['handlers']['task'] = {
    'class':
'airflow.utils.log.elasticsearch_task_handler.ElasticsearchTask
Handler',
    'formatter': 'airflow',
    'base_log_folder':
os.environ.get('AIRFLOW__LOGGING__BASE_LOG_FOLDER', '/
opt/airflow/logs'),
```

```
'log_id_template': '{dag_id}-{task_id}-{execution_date}-
{try_number}',

'filename_template': '{dag_id}/{task_id}/{execution_date}/
{try_number}.log',

'end_of_log_mark': 'end_of_log',

'es_kwargs': {

    'es_host': 'http://elasticsearch:9200',

    'log_id_template': '{dag_id}-{task_id}-{execution_date}-
{try_number}',

    'index_name': 'airflow-logs'

  }

}
```

- Deploy the ELK Stack services with Docker or Kubernetes

- Configure dashboards in Kibana to visualize logs by DAG, task, status, timestamp, or message

With this setup, each task execution sends logs directly to Elasticsearch, where they can be queried quickly and efficiently, even in environments with thousands of daily executions.

DAG Execution Auditing

Auditing in Airflow environments aims to track critical user actions such as:

- Creation, editing, or deletion of DAGs

- Manual execution triggers

- Pausing and resuming DAGs

- Modifying connections and variables

- Changes in access permissions (RBAC)

Although Airflow does not have a complete audit system by default, it is possible to implement custom audit logs using:

- Callback resources in DAGs (on_success_callback, on_failure_callback)

- Middleware in external systems connected via REST API

- Custom logging via specific audit operators

- Tracking changes in the metadata database

- Records in auxiliary tables using PythonOperator

Example using on_success_callback for audit logging:

python

```python
def register_success(context):
    dag_id = context['dag'].dag_id
    task_id = context['task'].task_id
    execution_date = context['execution_date']
    print(f'[AUDIT] DAG: {dag_id} | Task: {task_id} | Date: {execution_date}')


dag = DAG(
    dag_id='financial_pipeline',
    on_success_callback=register_success,
```

```
schedule_interval='@daily',
catchup=False
)
```

This automatically logs every successful execution, with the possibility of storing in a database, sending to an external API, or logging in Elasticsearch.

Log Retention and Rotation

Logs in data environments grow quickly. DAGs that run multiple times a day with dozens of tasks can generate hundreds of megabytes or gigabytes per week. Without a retention plan, local or remote storage can be compromised.

Best retention practices include:

- Define retention time by policy (e.g., 90 days for production, 30 days for dev)

- Rotate logs with tools like logrotate (in local environments)

- Configure lifecycle rules in S3/GCS buckets to automatically delete old logs

- Compress logs with gzip before upload (reduces storage costs)

- Automatically delete logs from test or debug DAGs

In Elasticsearch, rotation can be done via Index Lifecycle Management (ILM), configuring policies that delete or move old indexes.

Additionally, it is possible to include cleanup logic with

auxiliary DAGs:

python

```python
from airflow.operators.python import PythonOperator


def clean_logs(**kwargs):
    import shutil
    import os
    base_path = '/opt/airflow/logs'
    for root, dirs, files in os.walk(base_path):
        for d in dirs:
            # delete directories older than 60 days
            pass


task_cleanup = PythonOperator(
    task_id='clean_old_logs',
    python_callable=clean_logs,
    dag=dag
)
```

Common Error Resolution

Logs do not appear in the web interface
Check if the logs/ directory exists and has correct permissions.
For remote logging, check the remote_log_conn_id key.

Authentication error using Elasticsearch
Ensure the host is accessible, basic auth/token is correct, and indexing is enabled.

Overlapping or truncated logs
Can occur in environments with multiple workers sharing the log folder without isolation. Configure logs with a unique log_id_template per task.

Error integrating with GCS or S3
The connection must contain an access key and a bucket with read and write permission. Use airflow connections get to validate.

Failure reading remote log
Usually occurs when the log was not fully uploaded to the backend. Confirm remote_logging = True is active and that the upload happens on task_exit().

Best Practices

- Centralize logs in a remote backend (S3, GCS, ELK)

- Configure asynchronous logs for distributed environments

- Apply automatic compression (gzip) to reduce storage

- Create dashboards and alerts for error logs and critical failures

- Use indexing by DAG, task, and date for easier analysis

- Audit executions with callbacks and records in a database or APIs

- Implement retention with lifecycle rules in storage buckets

- Separate sensitive logs from operational logs (e.g.,

authentication data)

- Enable custom log_format for easier parsing by external tools

- Document the adopted logging and auditing strategy for all teams

Strategic Summary

An advanced logging system and efficient auditing are the foundation of observability, governance, and operational reliability in Apache Airflow data orchestration environments. Centralizing, protecting, visualizing, and controlling DAG and task logs is essential for quick diagnostics, failure prevention, regulatory compliance, and continuous pipeline improvement.

Integration with the ELK Stack, automating audit callbacks, applying retention policies, and using distributed log backends like S3 or Elasticsearch elevate Airflow to a professional operational level. By applying these strategies, the data engineer turns logs into a powerful tool for analysis, control, and operational evolution.

CHAPTER 24. REAL-WORLD ORCHESTRATION CASES WITH AIRFLOW

The maturity of a data operation is measured, among other factors, by the ability to orchestrate complex flows reliably, transparently, and scalably. Apache Airflow, in this context, has become the de facto standard in organizations of all sizes to control ingestion, transformation, load, validation, and data delivery pipelines. As solutions become more integrated, teams more specialized, and volumes more intense, Airflow's role expands beyond simple script execution: it consolidates itself as the operational nervous system of modern data engineering.

We will explore real-world orchestration cases with Airflow, highlighting strategies applied in ingestion and transformation pipelines, coexistence across multiple environments, team collaboration using centralized Airflow, critical flow standardization processes, as well as recurring production errors and the set of best practices that support resilient and auditable environments.

Ingestion and Data Transformation Pipeline

One of the most common applications of Airflow is orchestrating pipelines that ingest data from various sources (APIs, relational databases, files, events) and perform transformations before storing the results in a final destination (data warehouse, data lake, or analytical system).

Real example: e-commerce data ingestion

- The DAG starts with extracting sales orders via REST API from a platform like Shopify, Magento, or an internal platform.

- The data is temporarily saved in CSV or JSON files in a local directory or an S3 bucket.

- A validation task ensures that the files have the expected structure and volume.

- The transformation occurs with Spark, dbt, or SQL scripts, normalizing the data and enriching it with customer and product information.

- Finally, the data is loaded into a partitioned table in the data warehouse.

This typical flow can include operators such as:

- SimpleHttpOperator for API calls

- PythonOperator for transformations with Pandas or PySpark

- BashOperator for invoking external pipelines

- S3ToRedshiftOperator or BigQueryInsertJobOperator for final load

The DAG runs hourly, with tolerance windows and automatic backfill to cover previous failures. This model is replicable across multiple areas — finance, marketing, operations — simply by changing the sources and transformations.

Workflows with Multiple Environments

Mature data environments operate across different layers: development, staging, and production. Airflow allows isolating each environment physically (separate instances) or logically (same cluster with segregated DAGs and resources).

Applied scenario: data team in multiple environments

- Development environment runs locally with SQLite or PostgreSQL, only for unit tests.

- Staging environment simulates production, with reduced data volume and real connections.

- Production environment runs on Kubernetes with CeleryExecutor, storing logs in S3 and DAGs versioned in Git.

Each environment has:

- Git repository with distinct branches (e.g., develop, staging, main)

- Isolated variables and connections via AIRFLOW_HOME, secrets manager, or separate airflow.cfg files

- Deploy via CI/CD pipelines specific to each environment

The same DAG code can behave differently depending on the environment, using variables and conditionals:

python

```python
if Variable.get("env") == "staging":
    endpoint = "https://api-test.example.com"
else:
    endpoint = "https://api.example.com"
```

This strategy ensures production stability, reduces unexpected failures, and promotes safe testing with rapid feedback.

Integration Between Teams with Centralized Airflow

As different teams share the same Airflow cluster, it's essential to adopt strategies that allow collaboration without conflict, such as DAG segmentation, RBAC control, and queue isolation.

Real case: company with data team and marketing team

- Data team handles ingestion, transformation, and load DAGs.

- Marketing team orchestrates campaigns, lead synchronization, and real-time reports.

- Both teams share the same Airflow infrastructure with access via RBAC.

- Connections like postgres_default, api_marketing, crm_conn are shared with different permissions.

Each DAG is identified by owner, tags, and dag_id prefix, such as:

python

```
dag = DAG(
    dag_id='data_ingestion_orders',
    owner='data_engineering',
    tags=['data', 'etl'],
    ...
)
```

```
dag = DAG(
    dag_id='mkt_campaign_trigger',
    owner='marketing',
    tags=['mkt', 'webhook'],
    ...
)
```

This model allows governance to manage access, executions, and logs without one team directly impacting another's flow. Centralization also favors standardization, reuse of operators, and unified failure monitoring.

Standardization of Critical Flows

In production environments, some flows are considered critical: financial loads, regulatory reports, pricing updates, among others. For these cases, it's essential that DAGs follow a strict standard that includes:

- Input validation

- Post-processing consistency checks

- Error or delay notifications

- Automatic backup of input data

- Fault tolerance with retries, backoff, and configured catchup

Financial closing DAG

- Manual start by an authorized user or automatic trigger via API

- Extraction of accounts payable and receivable data

- Consolidation with daily exchange rates and taxes

- Balance validation and divergence with the previous day

- Export to PDF, spreadsheet, and digitally signed email

- Storage of evidence in versioned bucket

- Slack notification with a link to the report

Each stage has a dedicated operator, exclusive pool (e.g., finance), and priority queue (high_priority). Logs are exported to Elasticsearch, and executions are recorded in a compliance dashboard.

Common Error Resolution

DAG runs at the wrong time or with incorrect parameters

Check start_date, schedule_interval, and whether catchup is set correctly. DAGs with start_date=datetime.now() cause unpredictable behavior.

DAG error in multi-environment setup
Ensure variables, connections, and external dependencies are available in all environments. Use synchronized versioning.

Confusion between similarly named DAGs
Standardize DAG names with identifying prefixes (etl_, mkt_, rpt_) and use tags for filters in the interface.

DAG fails without apparent reason after change

Always use airflow tasks test or airflow dags test before pushing to production. Check full task logs.

Tasks don't run after manual trigger
The DAG may be paused. Validate via UI or airflow dags list command.

Best Practices

- Version all DAGs with Git, CI/CD, and mandatory review

- Test each new DAG with airflow tasks test and in staging environment

- Use Variable.get() with default_var to avoid failures due to missing variables

- Document each DAG with doc_md, tags, and a clear description in the code

- Organize DAGs into subfolders by domain: /dags/finance/, /dags/marketing/

- Monitor executions with alerts in Slack, PagerDuty, or Grafana dashboards

- Consolidate retry, timeout, pool, and queue patterns by DAG type

- Create a standard validation operator for all critical pipelines

- Avoid hardcoding — use environment variables, connections, and config files

- Store input and output data with versioning (e.g., s3://

bucket/etl/2024-06-01/input/)

Strategic Summary

Real-world orchestration cases with Apache Airflow show how the tool goes far beyond automating technical tasks. It connects departments, standardizes processes, enables governance over critical executions, and offers complete visibility into data in motion. In ingestion and transformation pipelines, Airflow acts as a conductor coordinating multiple services. In environments with different teams and domains, it provides a modular and segmented structure for safe collaboration. And in critical workflows, it enforces operational discipline with controlled logs, validations, and notifications.

CHAPTER 25. CONTINUOUS MONITORING AND OBSERVABILITY

Operating data pipelines with confidence requires more than scheduled runs and completed tasks. It's crucial to ensure continuous monitoring and full observability across the entire lifecycle of DAGs in Apache Airflow. In corporate environments, where multiple workflows directly impact financial operations, product deliveries, or executive dashboards, the absence of alerts, metrics, or centralized visibility can silently cause serious impacts.

The combination of health checks, smart notifications, collection of technical metrics, operational dashboards, and proactive failure resolution transforms Airflow from a reactive tool into a truly reliable and mature orchestration platform. This chapter presents in depth the pillars that support this model: active verification of DAG states, integration with alert systems (such as Slack, email, PagerDuty), metrics collection and exposure via Prometheus, visualization with Grafana, and best practices for uninterrupted operation.

DAG Health Checks

Health checks are automatic, periodic verifications that ensure a DAG is healthy—that is, running as expected, with no accumulated failures, not accidentally paused, and with tasks within the established SLA.

Common health check strategies:

- Auxiliary DAGs monitoring other DAGs

- PythonOperators with internal validation logic (e.g., expected execution counts)

- Internal APIs validating the last successful execution

- Execution probes via airflow dags list-runs and airflow tasks state

Example of a health check DAG:

python

```python
from airflow import DAG
from airflow.operators.python import PythonOperator
from airflow.utils.dates import days_ago
from airflow.models.dagrun import DagRun


def verify_execution():
    from airflow.utils.session import create_session
    from datetime import datetime, timedelta
    with create_session() as session:
        runs = session.query(DagRun).filter(
            DagRun.dag_id == 'etl_financeiro',
            DagRun.execution_date > datetime.utcnow() -
timedelta(hours=6),
            DagRun.state == 'success'
        ).count()
```

```python
    if runs == 0:
        raise Exception('DAG etl_financeiro failed in the last 6 hours')


dag = DAG('healthcheck_etl_financeiro',
start_date=days_ago(1), schedule_interval='@hourly')


check = PythonOperator(
    task_id='verify_etl_financeiro',
    python_callable=verify_execution,
    dag=dag
)
```

This DAG monitors another critical DAG and raises an error if no successful run is found in 6 hours. The health check failure can, in turn, trigger alerts.

Alerts via Email, Slack, PagerDuty

Airflow allows configuring automatic alerts for failure, timeout, or SLA violation via email, Webhook, or integration with external tools.

At the DAG level:

python

```python
from airflow.operators.email import EmailOperator


def failure_alert(context):
    EmailOperator(
```

```python
    task_id='send_alert',
    to='data@company.com',
    subject=f"Error in DAG {context['dag'].dag_id}",
    html_content=f"""
    Task {context['task'].task_id} failed.
    Execution date: {context['execution_date']}
    See more at: {context['task_instance'].log_url}
    """,
    dag=context['dag']
  ).execute(context)


dag = DAG('sales_pipeline', on_failure_callback=failure_alert)
```

Or with Slack:

python

```python
from airflow.providers.slack.operators.slack_webhook import
SlackWebhookOperator


def slack_alert(context):
    message = f"""
    *Error in DAG:* `{context['dag'].dag_id}`
    *Task:* `{context['task'].task_id}`
    *Date:* `{context['execution_date']}`
    *Log:* {context['task_instance'].log_url}
    """
```

```
alert = SlackWebhookOperator(
    task_id='slack_notification',
    http_conn_id='slack_default',
    message=message,
    channel='#monitoring',
)
alert.execute(context)
```

For more advanced integrations, such as PagerDuty, use PythonOperator with custom HTTP calls or libraries like pypd.

Airflow also allows alerts for SLA violations:

python

```
dag = DAG('etl_prices', default_args={'sla':
timedelta(minutes=30)}, sla_miss_callback=failure_alert)
```

Metrics with Prometheus

Airflow exposes internal metrics through the /metrics endpoint when the Prometheus component is enabled. These metrics include:

- Number of active DAGs

- Number of tasks per status (running, success, failed)

- Average execution time

- Task queue size

- Time between scheduling and execution

- Worker and scheduler health checks

To enable the exporter:

- Install the apache-airflow-providers-prometheus package

- Add to webserver_config.py:

python

```python
from prometheus_client import make_wsgi_app
from werkzeug.middleware.dispatcher import DispatcherMiddleware

from airflow.www.app import create_app

app = create_app()
application = DispatcherMiddleware(app, {
    '/metrics': make_wsgi_app()
})
```

- Configure Prometheus with a scrape on the /metrics endpoint

With this, Airflow metrics are continuously exported and can be visualized and analyzed by any Prometheus-compatible tool.

Dashboards with Grafana

With data collected via Prometheus, you can create highly visual and operational dashboards in Grafana, providing real-time visibility to analysts, engineers, and support teams.

Common dashboard components:

- Runs per DAG (last 24h, by status)

- Tasks with highest average duration

- Most failing tasks per DAG

- Number of DAGs queued or running simultaneously

- SLA violations per day

- Daily health check with semaphore (green/yellow/red)

The Airflow community offers ready-made Grafana dashboard templates with variables by DAG, task, worker, and status. With this, you can identify bottlenecks, detect anomalous behavior, and prevent failures before they cause real impact.

Dashboards should be integrated into NOC TV walls or dedicated Slack channels, reinforcing a culture of operational data and proactive action.

Common Error Resolution

Metrics don't appear in Prometheus
Check if the /metrics endpoint is correctly enabled. Check webserver logs for startup errors. Verify if the port is open.

Alerts don't trigger
There may be an error in DAG configuration (missing on_failure_callback) or missing token/authentication in Slack or SMTP connection. Validate webhook or email server permissions.

Logs lack useful information

Use logging.info() inside operators and avoid print(). Structure messages with context (dag_id, task_id, parameters).

Alerts with outdated data
Check if the used context is correct (execution_date, task_instance). Update message logic as needed.

Grafana shows incomplete data
Adjust Prometheus scrape_interval. Check if the exporter is active on all relevant nodes.

Best Practices

- Create health check DAGs monitoring critical DAGs

- Enable alert callbacks with detailed context

- Use SLA for tasks with strict execution windows

- Display Airflow dashboards on NOC or corporate TV screens

- Store all metrics in Prometheus and logs in Elasticsearch

- Centralize notifications in channels with escalation (Slack → PagerDuty)

- Automate alert tests by simulating periodic failures

- Log received alerts in a database or spreadsheet for recurrence analysis

- Train all technical teams to interpret dashboard data

- Review metrics weekly and adjust thresholds according to expected load

Strategic Summary

Continuous monitoring and observability are not accessories in a modern Apache Airflow operation—they are foundational elements of trust, governance, and scale. By combining automated health checks, smart alerts, exposed metrics, and visual dashboards, teams move from a reactive posture to a proactive engineering model.

Airflow, integrated with tools like Prometheus and Grafana, becomes a living platform where every DAG is monitored, every failure is detected, and every violation is recorded. This full visibility empowers engineers, reduces incidents, and strengthens the culture of reliability and transparency in data. By applying these practices, orchestration with Airflow stops being merely functional and becomes truly operational.

FINAL CONCLUSION

Throughout this technical and practical manual, we consolidated the most advanced foundations and strategies for data orchestration using Apache Airflow. This journey was carefully structured not only to present the tool's components but also to show how to apply them in real, professional, and critical contexts. Airflow is not just a task scheduler — it is a complete operational engineering platform where DAGs represent flows of decisions, data, and value.

Summary of Applied Technical Concepts

The structure of this book followed a didactic and modular progression. We started with local installation, moved to DAG creation, explored operators and internal components, connected Airflow with external systems, implemented scalable execution patterns, and finally structured observability and security strategies.

These concepts were accompanied by concrete practices with PythonOperator, BashOperator, SparkSubmitOperator, BranchPythonOperator, SimpleHttpOperator, among others. We studied trigger_rules, task_concurrency, start_date, catchup, pools, XCom, DAG params, sla, and callbacks as pillars for building reliable DAGs.

We advanced to production setups with Docker, Docker Compose, CeleryExecutor, KubernetesExecutor, and remote logging in S3, GCS, and ELK. Security was covered with RBAC, Fernet encryption, and protection of sensitive variables. Continuous operation was ensured with health checks, integrated alerts, and technical dashboards.

These are the practical foundations of an orchestration system that not only executes but operates autonomously, predictably, and audibly — this is, in essence, production engineering with Airflow.

Chapter-by-chapter summary

Chapter 1 – Getting Started with Apache Airflow
Local installation, directory structure, user creation, and scheduler/webserver startup. Clear operational introduction to DAG, task, scheduler, executor.

Chapter 2 – Creating Your First DAG
Basic DAG definition with PythonOperator, start_date, catchup, manual CLI execution, importance of organization and sequential chaining.

Chapter 3 – Essential Operators in Airflow
Analysis of core operators: BashOperator, PythonOperator, EmailOperator. Parameters, behavior, and task composition.

Chapter 4 – Working with Variables and Connections
Use of Variable.get(), credential protection, structuring connections via UI, use of conn_id and params for secure parameterization.

Chapter 5 – Trigger Rules and Dependencies
Execution rules like all_success, all_failed, all_done; applying conditional logic with trigger_rule in real workflows.

Chapter 6 – Scheduling and Execution Intervals

schedule_interval, cron expressions, timedelta, start_date vs. execution_date, catchup effects.

Chapter 7 – XComs: Task Communication
xcom_push(), xcom_pull() for inter-task data exchange, performance and serialization care.

Chapter 8 – Branching with BranchPythonOperator
Conditional execution using task_id return, branching logic, and flow consolidation with trigger_rule='none_skipped'.

Chapter 9 – Sensors: Monitoring External Conditions
FileSensor, HttpSensor, ExternalTaskSensor, poke and reschedule modes, timeout, worker impact.

Chapter 10 – Monitoring DAGs and Tasks
Web UI, detailed logs, graphical views, integration with external tools, duration and failure analysis.

Chapter 11 – Customizing Operators and Hooks
Creating custom BaseOperator and BaseHook, reusing logic, packaging modules, implementing corporate patterns.

Chapter 12 – Parallelism and Concurrency
parallelism, dag_concurrency, max_active_runs, task_concurrency, scaling executions without overloading workers.

Chapter 13 – Production Deployment with Docker
Airflow with Docker and Docker Compose, custom images, volumes, variables, deploy automation with pipelines.

Chapter 14 – Airflow with Kubernetes Executor
Deploy in Kubernetes clusters, pod templates, per-task isolation, autoscaling.

Chapter 15 – Orchestration with Spark and Hadoop
Integrating SparkSubmitOperator with HDFS, ETL pipelines with Spark and Hive, distributed logging, Hadoop sensors.

Chapter 16 – Integrations with APIs and Webhooks
SimpleHttpOperator for REST calls, payload delivery, endpoint consumption, external integrations.

Chapter 17 – Local Testing and DAG Debugging
airflow tasks test, print(), logging, VS Code breakpoints, execution validation with airflow dags test.

Chapter 18 – Jinja Templates and Macros
Use of {{ ds }}, {{ execution_date }}, macros.ds_add, dynamic command, path, and filter parameterization.

Chapter 19 – Security in Airflow
Authentication setup, RBAC, roles, variable protection, Fernet Key, secure practices with OAuth, LDAP, JWT.

Chapter 20 – Airflow REST API
Using GET, POST, DELETE on REST endpoints to trigger DAGs, create variables, integrate Airflow via automation.

Chapter 21 – DAG Versioning
Git control, environment-specific branches, CI/CD pipelines,

change audits, traceable deploys.

Chapter 22 – Scaling with Celery Executor
Distributed architecture, Redis and RabbitMQ brokers, performance tuning, dedicated queues, specialized workers.

Chapter 23 – Advanced Logging and Auditing
Centralized logs in S3, GCS, ELK, audit mechanisms, retention policies, traceability guarantees.

Chapter 24 – Real-World Orchestration Cases with Airflow
Ingestion pipelines, multi-environment setups, team integration, critical flow standardization with centralized Airflow.

Chapter 25 – Continuous Monitoring and Observability
Health checks, Slack and PagerDuty alerts, Prometheus metrics exposure, Grafana dashboards.

Recap of tools and workflows used

Key tools:

- Apache Airflow (Webserver, Scheduler, CLI)

- Docker, Docker Compose

- Kubernetes (Executor, pod templates, Helm)

- Git (DAG versioning)

- Redis, RabbitMQ (brokers)

- PostgreSQL, MySQL (metadatabase)

- Prometheus, Grafana (observability)

- Slack, Email, PagerDuty (notifications)

- ELK Stack, GCS, S3 (logging)

- Spark, HDFS, Hive (Big Data)

- REST APIs, Webhooks, OAuth (external integration)

Standard workflows included extraction, transformation, load, validation, alerts, conditional branching, reprocessing, versioning, automatic deploy.

Practical indications for professional application

This content was structured for immediate use in real environments. Any organization relying on data for operations can apply these concepts to:

- Reduce failures in critical pipelines

- Implement governance over data executions

- Ensure observability over flows and failures

- Automate data and report deliveries

- Integrate heterogeneous platforms via Webhooks and APIs

- Provide security and traceability for auditors and compliance

- Scale their data operation confidently

Airflow is used by companies like Airbnb, Netflix, PayPal, Mercado Libre, and thousands of organizations worldwide. The lessons here apply equally to startups and multinational infrastructures.

Practical Direction for

Advanced Apache Airflow Orchestration

With the fundamentals mastered, the next natural step is specialization in dynamic and contextual flows, such as:

- Business-line-parameterized DAGs

- Orchestration across multiple Airflow clusters

- Event-driven pipelines

- Reactive logic DAGs with context persistence

- Building DAG Factories

- Using TaskFlow API for typed and modularized DAGs

- Airflow with DataOps and MLOps

- Multicloud deploy with distributed observability

Additionally, mastering the REST API, CI/CD integration, and adapting Airflow to meet SLAs and corporate policies positions the data engineer as a critical infrastructure operator, capable of continuous delivery and constant innovation.

To the reader who made it here: thank you.

This book was written with the commitment to deliver practical, direct, and complete content on Apache Airflow

— not just as a tool, but as an instrument of operational transformation.

Every line, example, and practice shared was designed for you who seek technical excellence, structural mastery, and real impact in data engineering projects. May this content serve as a reference, springboard, and fuel for your professional journey.

Keep exploring, building, and orchestrating. With intelligence, rigor, and vision.

Sincerely,
Diego Rodrigues & Team!

www.ingramcontent.com/pod-product-compliance
Lightning Source LLC
LaVergne TN
LVHW022312060326
832902LV00020B/3420